How to
Survive
Your
Storm

Liston Page, Jr.

ISBN: 0-9755311-6-6

Published by

LIFEBRIDGE
BOOKS
P.O. BOX 49428
CHARLOTTE, NC 28277

Printed in the United States of America.

DEDICATION

I would like to dedicate this book to my parents, Bishop Liston Page, Sr., and Dr. Hazel Page. In my younger days I really thought you two were crazy: first for giving so much of yourselves as pastors and second for making me tag along! Then, as I began to mature, I still thought you were crazy, but I wasn't concerned because I didn't have to tag along any more. As time went on, even though I wasn't physically there, I know it was your love and prayers from a distance that kept me. You were able to look at me when I was high on drugs and see me through the eyes of God. As my friends walked away and my habits grew worse your prayers became stronger and your arms opened wider.

You believed in me and the anointing that was on me, even when I looked at life as if it were a joke. I thank you for being exactly what I needed—as parents, friends, pastors and now mentors. I thank God for you and the awesome responsibility you have charged me with as I pastor the church you founded and continue the legacy you started over twenty years ago. You have been consistent in your love and support of me.

Thanks for seeing me through the storm. I love you.

– Bishop Liston Page, II

CONTENTS

ACKNOWLEDGMENTS

With a humble and grateful heart, I first give honor and glory to my Lord and Savior Jesus Christ. Without Him there would be no life, and hence no storms to overcome. To the gift that has resulted in many, I thank God for my wife, partner and friend, Zelda Page, for being such a blessing to my life, our children, as well as our ministry. Thank you for truly exemplifying unconditional love to our children both natural and spiritual and, most importantly (smile) to me. The example you display of being a God-fearing wife, mother and partner in ministry has inspired me after twenty years of marriage, to become a greater husband, father, friend and pastor. I LOVE YOU Z!

To our children Krystal and Liston III, thanks for loving me and being so understanding as I have had to nurture others at the expense of fathering you. I know it hasn't always been fair or easy, but your love and support has been a model of how to survive the storm when it literally hits home. You are my inspiration and I TRULY DO LOVE YOU!

I would like to thank my parents Bishop Liston Page, Sr. and Dr. Hazel Page. It has been your example and leadership which has assisted me throughout the years. I would also like to thank all my Apostolic

Fathers: Bishop Andrew Merritt, Bishop Alfred A. Owens, Bishop Donald Hilliard, Bishop J. Delano Ellis, Bishop Don Meares, Bishop Kenneth Moales, Bishop Clifford Frazier, Bishop Eric Garnes, Bishop Larry Trotter, and Bishop William Washington for guiding me in my pursuit to be a humble servant, pastor and father. Your assistance and excellence has been a blessing to my life and ministry.

I thank God for blessing me with many friends and mentors in the Lord's work: Archbishop Roy and Paula Brown, Bishop Paul and Debra Morton, Rev. Dr. Frank and Marla Reid, Rev. Dr. Floyd and Elaine Flake, Bishop Walter Scott and Patricia Thomas, Bishop Eric and Subrenia McDaniel, Bishop Neil and Patrice Ellis, Superintendent J. Drew and Karen Sheard, Bishop George and Mary Searight, Pastors Randy and Paula White, Dr. Paul and Jan Crouch, Bishop-Designate Mitchell & Barbara Taylor, Pastor Lester and Franciane Love, Bishop Noel Jones, Bishop T.D. and Serita Jakes, Pastor Jentezen Franklin, Rev. Jamaal Bryant, Dr. Dana and Rachelle Carson, Pastor Milton Biggham and Bishop Michael and Rhonda Ford. Your prayers, encouragement, mentorship and hospitality throughout the years have meant more to me than I could ever express.

I would like to extend a special thanks to two very good friends of mine and their wives. First, to Bishop Darryl and Dionne Brister—for the inspiration and information you have poured into my life to ensure that this long awaited vision could come forth. If it had not been for your commitment and dedication to the study of God's Word, you would not have been able to impart in me the biblical truths and illuminations needed to complete this book. I will forever be indebted and grateful for the friendship we both share. And, second, Bishop Shelton and Kim Bady; I thank God for connecting us in this very crucial time. You have truly exemplified what a great ministry is all about. Your outpouring of excellence and your desire to see the kingdom grow has truly taken us to the next level. God Bless You for the partnership!

I send much love and appreciation to my administrative staff, Paul Sexton, Mark Foxworth, Kevin Moses, Takeisha Reels, Shelley Silverman, and Alan P. Walker. Thank you for your faithfulness, and your hand in bringing forth the vision God has given me. I would also like to thank my church leaders, both past and present, Pastor Reggie and Loretta Hall, Elder Michael Odom, Deacon Freddie Kelly and Deacon Thomas Chestnut for their outstanding fervor and commitment to this ministry throughout the past eight years. And a special thanks to Pastor Jeffrey and Drusilla White. I praise God for the growth and many blessings which have transpired in my life and the lives of our entire church family throughout my tenure as Pastor. I know this has all been possible as a result of faithful, prayerful men and women who have kept my family and I lifted up and well taken care of. Thanks for allowing me to be me (smile), as I pastor, befriend, and love each and every one of you. Thank you Highway Church and I look forward to everything God has in store for us!

Last, but not least, I would like to thank my brother, Pastor Darren Page, and my sister, Wanda Page. I didn't forget you. I want to say I love you and pray God's best for you and your families. Thanks for everything—and keep surviving the storms!

– Bishop Liston Page, Jr.

FOREWORD

When I first heard that my son, Liston Page, Jr., was writing a book with the title *HOW TO SURVIVE YOUR STORM,* I smiled and said to myself, "He is certainly an authority on the subject!"

I wish I could tell you Liston, our eldest son, was a perfect child who never strayed from the path, but this is not the case. It is impossible to count the times my wife, Hazel, and I spent sleepless nights on our knees asking the Lord to guard, protect and deliver our son from "the snare of the fowler."

God was faithful and our prayers were answered beyond anything we could ask or think. Not only did he totally commit his life to the Lord, but followed the call to full time ministry. Words cannot describe my emotions when, after pastoring the Highway Church in Patterson, NJ, for 27 years, I was able to turn the pulpit over to my son. Even more, I rejoice that I was able to participate in the consecration service where he became *Bishop* Liston Page, Jr.

Life-Changing Principles

As you read this book, please understand it is not

written by someone on the outside looking in. It is a powerful book for two reasons: First, the author has been there! Second, it is based on a knowledge of the Word of God which has been forged by serious study and ignited by the Holy Spirit.

It makes no difference whether the problem you face is a small dark cloud or a full-blown storm. The principles you will discover on these pages will allow you to find a solid rock on which you can safely stand.

Equally important, you will understand the reason the Almighty allows us to encounter the problems of life.

The Solutions You Need

In my years as a pastor, I have counseled with men and women who found themselves in the midst of situations beyond imagination—a mother whose son was brutally murdered in an alley near her home—a young man who slashed his wrists while high on drugs—a teenage girl who had been raped and was now pregnant.

Living in New York, I also know what it means to see an entire city shaken to its core when on September 11, 2001, terrorists flew two passenger jets into the World Trade Towers and killed thousands of innocent people. The carnage was beyond belief.

In an instant, without warning, any of us can

suddenly be faced with a crisis that leaves us crying for help.

Here is a message I wish could be placed into the hands of millions of people. It doesn't just ask questions, but offers answers needed for the distress they are facing—or will some day experience.

Let me encourage you to give copies of *HOW TO SURVIVE YOUR STORM* to those you love—friends and family members who need to find peace in their time of turmoil.

Someone once asked me, "Bishop, why do you believe the Bible?" I answered, "Because I know the Author!"

For the same reason I can recommend this book—I am more than well acquainted with the man who wrote it. This is a message which can literally save your life.

– Bishop Liston Page, Sr.

INTRODUCTION

It is not merely by chance you are holding this book in your hands. As sure as there is a God in heaven, I believe there's divine connection—even a special *timing*—involved with the Lord inspiring me to write these words and allowing you to receive them.

At this moment you may be confronting a crisis that is causing a troubled spirit, sleepless nights and perhaps physical pain. It may involve financial hardships, a doctor's negative report or a personal relationship which is tottering on the verge of collapse.

Just as in the rating system designed by the National Hurricane Center, the storm by which you are being battered may be a Category One, even a Category Five—an absolute catastrophe. Regardless of the severity, every tempest inflicts personal distress and threatens your well being.

There's Hope

My friend, don't feel frightened and alone when you are being chased by an emotional tsunami and are desperately scrambling to find higher ground. As scripture tells us, we *all* face storms from the day we enter this world, for *"man is born to trouble, as the sparks fly upward"* (Job 5:7).

However, just because we were birthed into difficulty doesn't mean we are destined to stay in such a condition. As the psalmist writes, *"Many are the afflictions of the righteous, but the Lord delivers him out of them all"* (Psalm 34:19).

Finding Answers

I can hardly wait for you to begin this journey with me. You're going to learn that while howling winds and raging seas pose a threat, they are often *necessary*.

Not only will you find the answers for your situation, I believe the spiritual knowledge you are about to acquire will help you share hope to those you love.

On these pages you'll discover:

- How to recognize the four storms of life.
- Five choices which can sink you spiritual ship.
- The key to restoring those who have fallen.
- The danger of creating your own tempest.
- How to avoid stirring up a whirlwind.
- The value of small storms in preparing you for a crisis.
- Where to find shelter in midst of the thunder.

- The path to deliverance in your darkest hour.
- Where to turn when you don't have the answer.
- How your vision can become a reality.
- The secret of defeating Satan's schemes.
- How to soar above your storm.

My friend, I am praying these words will penetrate your spirit and inspire you to not just *survive*, but to *thrive!*

That's why I can say with confidence, "Get ready! The sun is about to break through your clouds and shine!"

– Liston Page, Jr.

CHAPTER 1

THE FOUR
STORMS OF LIFE

E very spring we pick up the newspaper and find
a headline that reads, "Hurricane Forecasters Predict
Major Storms This Year."

How can the experts be so sure violent winds will
blow? Because they arrive *every* year—usually between June and November. Why only then? Because it
is the hurricane *season*.

Our time here on earth is not much different. There
are seasons of our lives when dark clouds gather and
our problems seem to intensify. It's part of human
experience.

Instead of asking, "Why am I going through this
valley?" or "What is God trying to teach me?" most
people, with a defeatist attitude, shrug their shoulders
and say, "All problems are out of my control. There
isn't much I can do about them."

Such carnal thinking represents a *stronghold*—a mindset which accepts a circumstance as inevitable and unchangeable, even if the conclusion goes against the will of God or is in contrast to your preordained destiny.

Mighty Weapons

Friend, you must deal with your storm because you can't allow Satan to manipulate your mind and magnify what you are going through.

As you will discover in this book, the Almighty can change the most dire situation in which you find yourself. As the apostle Paul declared: *"For the weapons of our warfare are not carnal but mighty in God for pulling down strongholds"* (2 Corinthians 10:4).

THE LIGHTNING MAY FLASH AND THE THUNDER ROLL, YET REMEMBER YOU ARE NOT ALONE.

The lightning may flash and the thunder roll, yet remember you are not alone. I love the words of the psalmist: *"The Lord has been mindful of us; He will bless us; He will bless the house of Israel; He will bless the house of Aaron. He will bless those who fear the Lord, both small and great. May the Lord give you increase more and more, you and your children"* (Psalm 115:13-14).

Still, you may question, "If God is *mindful* of us

and wants to *bless* and *increase* us, why does He allow storms to buffet the lives of His children?"

In answering this question we need to look at the *nature* of difficulty and distress. Just like hurricanes, all life's storms are not the same—they are ranked according to category and strength.

Understanding the *source* of the problem is the key to unlocking the solution. Let me help you recognize the four storms which interrupt every life:

1. NORMAL STORMS— CAUSED BY MOTHER NATURE

There are certain disturbances you simply cannot avoid. If you read your insurance policy closely, you'll discover some calamities the premiums will not cover. They are usually referred to as "an act of God."

As sure as the Creator *"makes His sun rise on the evil and on the good, and sends rain on the just and on the unjust"* (Matthew 5:45), you *will* experience turmoil.

Just before Jesus was arrested, placed on trial and crucified, He told His disciples, *"Indeed the hour is coming, yes, has now come, that you will be scattered, each to his own, and will leave Me alone. And yet I am not alone, because the Father is with Me. These things I have spoken to you, that in Me you may have peace. In the world you will have tribulation; but be of good* cheer, *I have overcome the world"* (John 16:31-33).

The Lord didn't say you "might" experience tribulation; He said *"you will!"*

Yet, despite the upheaval—from whatever source it may come—Jesus tells you to *"be of good cheer."*

Since there are natural situations which are unavoidable, take a deep breath and relax. Everything rests in God's capable hands.

2. STORMS WE ENGINEER THROUGH OUR FOOLISHNESS

If you choose to wander outside the will of God, you're headed for troubled waters.

Let me remind you what happened to Jonah. The Lord spoke to him, saying, *"Arise, go to Nineveh, that great city, and cry out against it; for their wickedness has come up before Me"* (Jonah 1:1-2).

Afraid of what may be waiting ahead, he rebelled. Jonah stood to his feet and began to run from the Lord. Scripture records, *"He went down to Joppa, and found a ship going to Tarshish; so he paid the fare, and went down into it, to go with them to Tarshish from the presence of the Lord"* (v.3).

What a disastrous decision! He had no idea of the trouble he was about to face. Aboard the ship, *"the Lord sent out a great wind...and there was a mighty tempest on the sea, so that the ship was about to be broken up"* (v.4).

A Vital Lesson

This story is a stern warning for you and me. We simply can't ignore the voice of the Lord and attempt to set our own agenda.

However, as the account unfolds, we learn that just because God places us in danger does not mean we will be totally destroyed. Some storms happen because the Lord wants our unwavering attention and can't get it any other way.

Jonah learned his lesson! Now inside the belly of the whale which swallowed him, he repented: *"I cried out to the Lord because of my affliction, and He answered me. Out of the belly of Sheol I cried, and You heard my voice. For You cast me into the deep, into the heart of the seas, and the floods surrounded me; all Your billows and your waves passed over me. Then I said, 'I have been cast out of Your sight; yet I will look again toward Your holy temple'"* (Jonah 2:2-4).

> **SOME STORMS HAPPEN BECAUSE THE LORD WANTS OUR UNWAVERING ATTENTION AND CAN'T GET IT ANY OTHER WAY.**

Not only did the whale vomit Jonah onto dry ground, he preached the Word to the people of Nineveh and the city of 120,000 turned from their evil ways (Jonah 3:10).

23

3. THE STORMS GOD SENDS FOR OUR SPIRITUAL DEVELOPMENT OR MATURITY

A man recently asked me, "Pastor, I'm living for the Lord as best I know how and believe I am in the center of His will, so why am I having such great trials and tests?"

I AM CONVINCED GOD PLACES CHALLENGES IN OUR PATH TO PRODUCE CHARACTER AND FORGE OUR FAITH.

I am convinced God places challenges in our path to shape our character and forge our faith. The fact you have been allowed to experience turmoil should let you know God *trusts* you—and believes you will grow spiritually in the process.

This type of storm is not designed to make you cry and feel sorry for yourself. No. It is meant to prod you to use the grit and tenacity necessary to exercise your faith.

Asleep in the Storm

Once, after preaching to the multitudes on the shore of Galilee, Jesus decided to cross over to the other side of the sea with His disciples. He was in one vessel, and *"other little boats were also with Him"* (Mark 5:36).

Suddenly, *"a great windstorm arose, and the waves beat into the boat, so that it was already filling. But He was in the stern, asleep on a pillow. And they awoke Him and said to Him, 'Teacher, do You not care that we are perishing?'"*(vv.37-38).

Jesus arose and rebuked the wind, saying to the sea, *"Peace, be still!"* (v.39).

Instantly the howling wind subsided and there was a great calm. Then Jesus questioned, *"Why are you so fearful? How is it that you have no faith?"* (v.40).

The terrified disciples asked each other, *"Who can this be, that even the wind and the sea obey Him!"* (v.41).

These men were walking with Jesus, yet He had to send them through a raging storm in order for them to capture the full revelation of who He was. It also energized their faith.

"Do Not Be Afraid"

On another occasion, just after the miraculous feeding of the five thousand, when *"Jesus perceived that they were about to come and take Him by force to make Him king, He departed again to the mountain by Himself alone"* (John 6:15).

When dusk fell, the disciples went down to the Sea of Galilee where they got into a boat and set off across the lake toward Capernaum. As scripture records, *"It was already dark, and Jesus had not come to them. Then the sea arose because a great wind was blowing. So when they had rowed about three or four miles, they saw Jesus walking on the sea and drawing near the boat; and they were afraid. But He said to them, 'It is I; do not be afraid'"* (vv.17-20).

In Matthew's account of the story, Peter answered Him and said, *"Lord, if it is You, command me to come to You on the water"* (Matthew 14:28).

Jesus said, *"Come."*

Peter confidently stepped out of the boat, walked on the water and came toward Jesus. *"But when he saw that the wind was boisterous, he was afraid; and beginning to sink he cried out, saying, 'Lord, save me!'"* (v.30).

Immediately, Jesus stretched out His hand, caught him and said, *"O you of little faith, why did you doubt?"* (v.31).

When they climbed back into the boat, the wind ceased and the vessel safely reached the shore where they were headed.

Don't Look at the Sea

It's important to realize this tempest arose in the darkest hours, yet Jesus was there. He *never* leaves us. If we fail to see the Son of God in the storm—when it is He who orchestrates it—we will never learn the intended lesson. He wants you to recognize, "This is not Satan. This is Me!"

When you are in a God-induced storm, regardless of the elements, if you keep your eyes on Jesus you will not drown. The water may be rising and the gale may blow, but you will never sink.

DON'T GIVE THE DEVIL CREDIT FOR SOMETHING NOT OF HIS MAKING.

Are you able to identify a difficulty sent by God to build your life? Don't give the devil credit for something not of his making.

4. THE STORMS THAT COME BECAUSE WE ARE CONNECTED TO THE WRONG PEOPLE

The problems many face are a direct result of making foolish choices regarding who they associate with. Their life is in constant turmoil because of wrong relationships.

Before long they are pouring out their hearts to these so-called friends and receiving flawed advice.

Friendship does not need to be based on revealing intimate secrets to one another. How much better to take it to the Lord in prayer. As I told my congregation, "We have too many folk running their mouth instead of getting on their knees!"

Remember this: Well-intentioned people may give

you bad advice, but the Lord never will!

God is not an author of confusion; He is the author of peace. It is the devil who comes to separate and divide. Make certain the counsel you receive from others is meant to calm your storm, not whip it up into a tornado.

ANYONE WHO HAS YOU LIE, CONNIVE OR CHEAT CANNOT HAVE YOUR BEST INTEREST AT HEART.

I've witnessed believers who become so close to an individual they can't distinguish between what is good or evil. As a result they follow wrong advice and find themselves out of God's will.

Anyone who encourages you to lie, connive or cheat cannot have your best interest at heart. Your so-called confidant may actually be a devil—yet you are so close you cannot see the handwriting on the wall.

We allow some people to do so much for us that we become reliant, even "embedded" to them in their foolishness. I've watched positive believers develop negative attitudes simply because of the pessimistic people with whom they spend the majority of their time.

Choose your friends prayerfully and wisely.

Not "Business as Usual"

There are consequences for ignoring godly advice.

When Paul was sentenced and handed over to a Roman centurion, they sailed for Rome. However, the boats on which they journeyed were far behind schedule because the winds would not allow them to stay on course. As the Bible states, *"Now when much time had been spent, and sailing was now dangerous because the Fast was already over"* Acts 27:9).

This was referring to the Jewish Day of Atonement which fell in the latter part of September or October. This was a day of fasting—a time of crucifying your flesh.

I can tell you from personal experience, when you complete a fast and are trying to become more like Jesus, the devil will throw every disturbance imaginable in your direction. This is not a time for "business as usual" because your physical man is not strong enough to fight demonic warfare. You need to strengthen yourself through prayer and receive direction from God.

According to biblical scholars, the usual sailing season in that part of the world lasted from Pentecost (May-June) to Tabernacles—which was five days following the Fast. Even the Romans considered a voyage after mid-September too dangerous. It was the start of the high storms.

Paul spoke up and advised, *"Men, I perceive that this voyage will end with disaster and much loss, not only of the cargo and ship, but also our lives"* (v.10).

However, Paul was a prisoner, and didn't have the final word. As the Bible tells us, *"the centurion was more persuaded by the helmsman and the owner of the ship than by the things spoken by Paul"* (v.11).

Whose Advice are You Heeding?

As strange as it seems, I've known Christians in the church who would rather take advice from worldly people than listen to the counsel of a saint of God.

Instead of heeding the words of Paul, they listened to the "majority." As scripture says: *"And because the harbor was not suitable to winter in, the majority advised to set sail from there also, if by any means they could reach Phoenix, a harbor of Crete opening toward the southwest and northwest, and winter there* (v.12).

Far too often we make hasty decisions because we don't like the conditions in which God places us. We are impatient—not willing to wait for the storm to pass.

Keep reading Acts 27 and you'll understand the consequences of wrong advice. The ship took such a violent battering on the sea they actually threw the cargo overboard. Hungry, cold and dejected, these men were shipwrecked 14 days later, surviving only by holding onto pieces of the wrecked ship and coming ashore at Malta.

If only they had listened to the man of God!

Recognize the Reason

Take a serious look at the crisis you are facing and ask yourself:

- Is it a normal storm over which you have no control?
- Has it been engineered by your own foolishness?
- Has it been sent by the Lord for your spiritual growth?
- Is it the result of being connected to the wrong people?

When you recognize the *reason* for the turmoil, with God's help you are on your way to a brighter day.

CHAPTER 2

DON'T SINK YOUR SPIRITUAL SHIP!

The Mediterranean tempest which battered and wrecked the ship carrying the apostle Paul to Rome was tangible—not a figment of his imagination. And the turmoil and persecution he would face for the remainder of his ministry was just as real.

Today, you and I are sailing in vessels that must be sea-worthy and storm-proof. Satan himself is out to thrust his arrows into our hull—and unless we are constantly on guard, our boat will not only spring a leak, we will be in danger of sinking.

Suddenly, we will be crying with the psalmist, *"Deliver me out of the mire, and let me not sink; and let me be delivered...out of the deep waters"* Psalm 69:14).

To avoid this situation, pay attention to these five warnings:

1

YOU WILL SINK YOUR SPIRITUAL SHIP
BY MAKING A DECISION IN HASTE

I've met people who, after a run-in with their boss, fueled with anger, quit their job on the spot—not realizing the same employer would one day be called for a job reference. Likewise, there are young people who have a confrontation with a high school teacher and become a statistic—a permanent drop out—limiting their future options.

What's the hurry?

Decisions made in haste almost always backfire. That is why we need to harness our human emotion and make choices based on God's direction and His schedule.

In the story of Paul's shipwreck, we see the danger of acting out of panic instead of waiting for the right moment. The captain of the ship was concerned that *"much time had been spent"* (Acts 27:9) and they were far behind schedule. Foolishly, he became over-anxious and sailed into stormy waters.

The Bible tells us there is a time and a season for everything—*"A time to be born, and a time to die; A time to plant, and a time to pluck what is planted...A time to weep, and a time to laugh; A time to mourn, and a time to dance...A time to keep silence, and a time to speak"* (Eccesiastes 3:2,4,7).

Perhaps the years are racing by and you're in a rush to get things done. Don't panic. Ask God to give you both patience and timing. In the words of David, *"Wait on the Lord; Be of good courage, and He shall strengthen your heart; Wait, I say, on the Lord!"* (Psalm 27:14).

2

YOU WILL SINK YOUR SPIRITUAL SHIP

BY DEPENDING ON WORLDLY ADVICE RATHER THAN THE WISDOM OF GOD

It baffles me when I see Bible-believing, God-fearing Christians run to the world for counsel and advice. Why would anyone follow the direction of a person who doesn't have a spiritual foundation? What is the value of listening to a man or woman who has no concept of the will of God for your life?

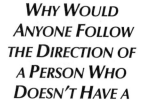

WHY WOULD ANYONE FOLLOW THE DIRECTION OF A PERSON WHO DOESN'T HAVE A SPIRITUAL FOUNDATION?

Find the *right* individual to give you the *right* information. As Solomon wrote: *"The thoughts of the righteous are right, but the counsels of the wicked are deceitful"* (Proverbs 12:5).

If you are unsure who to talk with, get on your knees and ask the Lord for direction. He will lead you to someone who can give sound advice. Then, after receiving wisdom, go to God's Word for confirmation. Don't make a move until the counsel you obtain lines up with scripture and you feel totally at peace in your heart.

3

You Will Sink Your Spiritual Ship By Taking the Easy Way Out

Relationships take time to mature and blossom. It takes months and even years to develop respect, confidence and trust in each other—as opposed to being quick to judge your partner for what he or she might have said or done. You don't just "get along" after being married.

We have to *work* on relationships at home, at church, in our community and on our job, never taking the quick, easy way out.

Jesus addresses this issue when He tells us if we have "ought" against someone, instead of spreading the story, go to the individual who hurt your feelings. Deal with the matter directly. Otherwise, the problem will grow like a thorny weed and become out of control.

In the words of Jesus, *"Moreover if your brother sins against you, go and tell him his fault between you*

and him alone. If he hears you, you have gained your
brother"* (Matthew 18:15).

If a brother has offended you, I trust you will love
him enough to seek him out and tell him personally,
"You have hurt my feelings. Can we talk this out?"

What if the individual refuses to listen? Jesus says
you are to *"take with you one or two more, that by the
mouth of two or three witnesses every word may be
established"* (v.16).

This doesn't mean you should recruit two or three
of your buddies or cohorts. No. Ask men or women of
God who know how to pray.

Gossip and criticism spoken behind an individual's
back has no place in the body
of Christ. If I were to repeat
everything said about members
of our church, I wouldn't have
one person left in the
congregation!

In the midst of conflict, it is
important to know who you are

*IN THE MIDST OF
CONFLICT IT IS
IMPORTANT TO
KNOW WHO YOU
ARE IN GOD.*

in God. If you are saved and delivered, you can rest in
the assurance there is favor on your life.

Personally, I refuse to take the easy way out
because the Lord has invested too much of the
anointing in me. It would be foolish to turn back now.

4

YOU WILL SINK YOUR SPIRITUAL SHIP
BY FOLLOWING THE CROWD

God asked Moses to send twelve men to secretly explore the land of Canaan. When these "spies" returned, ten of them gave a negative report. Yes, they saw the land flowing with milk and honey, but they also brought back an account of giants in the land. They planted fear in the hearts of the children of Israel when they said, *"the people who dwell in the land are strong; the cities are fortified and very large"* (Numbers 13:28). And they added, *"There we saw the giants...and we were like grasshoppers in our own sight, and so we were in their sight"* (v.33).

Just two of the spies, Joshua and Caleb, gave a positive report, saying, *"Let us go up at once and take possession, for we are well able to overcome it"* (v.30).

Who did the people listen to? They followed the pessimistic majority. That same night *"the congregation lifted up their voices and cried...And all the children of Israel complained against Moses and Aaron, and the whole congregation said to them, 'If only we had died in the land of Egypt! Or if only we had died in this wilderness! Why has the Lord brought*

us to this land to fall by the sword, that our wives and
children should become victims? Would it not be better
for us to return to Egypt?' So they said to one another,
'Let us select a leader and return to Egypt'" (Numbers
4:1-4).

It was the beginning of the end. The seeds sown by
a negative report caused the
Israelites to die in the
wilderness. Only Joshua and
Caleb entered the Promised
Land.

Stop listening to the crowd!
Stand up and declare, "Greater
is He who is in me than he who
is in the world!"

> *STAND UP AND
> DECLARE, "GREATER
> IS HE WHO IS IN ME
> THAN HE WHO IS IN
> THE WORLD!"*

5

YOU WILL SINK YOUR SPIRITUAL SHIP
BY DEPENDING ON THE CIRCUMSTANCES

The ship on which you are traveling may look
sturdy and powerful, yet anything made by man cannot
be trusted. As Hezekiah told the people when the king
of Assyria came to invade Judah, *"With him is an arm
of flesh; but with us is the Lord our God to help us and
to fight our battles"* (2 Chronicles 32:8).

Circumstances are immaterial when the King of
Kings is on your side. I love the words of David:

"Some trust in chariots, and some in horses: but we will remember the name of the Lord our God" (Psalm 20:7 KJV).

When dark clouds appear on the horizon, stand on God's Word: *"We are hard-pressed on every side, yet not crushed; we are perplexed, but not in despair; persecuted, but not forsaken; struck down, but not destroyed"* (2 Corinthians 4:8-9).

Now you are prepared for whatever is about to happen!

CHAPTER 3

"I'VE FALLEN AND I CAN'T GET UP!"

Would you like to know the quickest, shortest exit from your storm? Here it is! Find someone who is mired in a crisis and give them a helping hand.

The moment you stop wallowing in self-pity and begin to aid and assist another person, you are actually helping yourself. Why? Because your are now in the business of *restoration* instead of *desperation!*

This is not simply the opinion of Liston Page, Jr., but the admonition of the apostle Paul to the believers in Galatia.

Before sharing his thoughts on this pivotal principle, let me tell you why it is vital that *every* standard and practice for your life be backed by scripture.

"Living Testimonies"
Even though the Bible may be read by Christians

41

and sinners alike, it is primarily written to the church—to believers. The world's way of thinking cannot understand the Holy Bible, they can only dissect it from a humanistic viewpoint. This is a spiritual document, not a book to be read like a novel. It was written for a particular purpose and need—and becomes both our road map and a mirror as we reflect on the nature and character of God.

The Bible was given so that we (followers of Christ) can become living testimonies. As Paul writes: *"You are our epistle written in our hearts, known and read by all men; clearly you are an epistle of Christ, ministered by us, written not with ink but by the Spirit of the living God, not on tablets of stone but on tablets of flesh, that is, of the heart"* (2 Corinthians 3:2-3).

Piercing the Soul

Look into the Word to see if you reflect what scripture is saying. As long as you live on terra firma in this physical body, with an Adamic nature, you will constantly need God's Word to crucify your flesh.

Paul says, *"I die daily"* (1 Corinthians 15:31). This is only possible when you decide to stop conforming to the world and are *transformed* by the renewing of your mind. For, *"the word of God is living and powerful, and sharper than any two-edged sword, piercing even to the division of soul and spirit, and of joints and marrow, and is a discerner of the thoughts and intents of the heart"* (Hebrews 4:12).

The reason sinners cannot understand the Bible is because *"the natural man does not receive the things of the Spirit of God, for they are foolishness to him; nor can he know them, because they are spiritually discerned. But he who is spiritual judges all things"* (1 Corinthians 2:14-15).

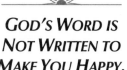

GOD'S WORD IS NOT WRITTEN TO MAKE YOU HAPPY, IT IS DESIGNED AS A PROCESS TO MAKE YOU HOLY.

God's Word is not written to make you happy, it is designed as a process to make you *holy.* Scripture teaches consecration and sanctification—to set us apart for the service of the Lord.

For Every Believer

When Paul addressed the issue of restoring a fallen brother, he was not writing to a specific individual, but to the entire church.

The book of Galatians is an epistle to the believers scattered throughout a region of Asia minor—now known as Turkey. There were congregations of Christ-followers in towns including Antioch, Lystra and Derbe. In fact, this is the only letter Paul writes to be circulated to *all* the churches in this particular region called Galatia.

This is important because it tells us these are not new issues to the church. Even more, Paul's counsel to first century believers addresses the same ills we struggle with today.

Repaired and Restored!

In this life-shaping letter, the apostle writes: *"Brethren, if a man is overtaken in any trespass, you who are spiritual restore such a one in a spirit of gentleness, considering yourself lest you also be tempted"* (Galatians 6:1).

Since restoration is critical in the life of every child of God, we should have the attitude to repair and restore—not just ourselves, but to see other lives mended. Even more, we are to grieve when one of our brothers or sisters falls from God's grace. From the depths of our soul we should desire to see the individual restored so they can function fully in the body of Christ.

When we encounter someone who has made a mistake, it is not because they want to live their lives in misery. On the contrary, they may be under a severe attack of the enemy—and because they do not associate or align themselves with praying people, cannot ward off the devil for themselves.

This is where you and I enter the picture. Such

individuals are desperately seeking help and we need to come to their rescue.

Unfortunately, some Christians judge others based on their own classification of the sin. They have created a "scale" and rank the offenses from minor infractions to major transgressions. Yet, the Bible says we are to restore *any* trespass (Galatians 6:1).

WE HAVE MORE "BONE BREAKERS" THAN "BONE SETTERS!"

The original meaning of "restore" is to mend or repair—even to set a broken bone back in place. Sadly, one of our problems is we have more "bone breakers" than "bone setters!"

A Needed Covering

The word "overtaken" means a person has been caught in a fault—or, as we like to say today, "busted!" A man becomes so caught up in sin he is "desensitized" to his iniquity and is walking outside of fellowship.

I believe "getting caught" is an expression of grace. After all, when you become calloused to the sin you are committing you need God to give you a wake up call and expose your transgressions.

Read the story of Noah and you'll discover that on one occasion he drank the wine from his vineyard and became so drunk he was lying naked in his tent. *"And Ham, the father of Canaan, saw the nakedness of his father, and told his two brothers outside"* (Genesis 9:22). They found a garment to cover his body.

Before this incident, Noah never allowed anyone in

his tent to look at his unclothed body—not even his own sons.

SIN WILL CAUSE US TO BECOME SO INTOXICATED WE CANNOT MAKE RATIONAL DECISIONS.

The strong drink impaired his judgment and brought him shame.

Sin will cause us to become so intoxicated we cannot make rational decisions. For this reason, when you are overtaken in a fault, you need someone to cover you.

Don't Isolate Yourself

We can learn much from the story in the Old Testament of David's perverted son, Amnon. In the account, Amnon knew how to manipulate people—and take advantage of his innocent virgin sister, Tamar.

Amnon pretended to be sick and asked Tamar to prepare him some food. On arrival, she placed a meal before him, but he refused to eat.

Then Amnon said, *"Have everyone go out from me"* (2 Samuel 13:9). When they did, he asked Tamar, *"Bring the food into the bedroom, that I may eat from your hand"* (v.10).

Obediently, Tamar took the cakes she had prepared and brought them to her brother in the bedroom. Next, Amnon grabbed her and demanded, *"Come, lie with me, my sister"* (v.11).

Even though the young woman protested, he raped her (v.14).

The crux of the matter is that Amnon isolated his sister from those who could help her.

"Bolt the Door!"

I see parallels to this story in the church. Because of someone's intent, you become sequestered from those who can assist you. Suddenly, you are being taken advantage of.

In some instances, you are treated like Tamar. After being violated, Amnon kicked her out of the house and ordered his servant: *"Here! Put this woman out, away from me, and bolt the door behind her"* (v.17).

What a feeling of utter despair when you don't have someone who knows the Lord to speak words of restoration into your life. It is tragic, even overwhelming, when an immature believer learns of your faults and has neither the wisdom or the spiritual knowledge to meet your need.

I can tell you from personal experience, there will come a time when you will require a seasoned saint who is mature enough in faith to pray you back to spiritual health. It does not matter what position you hold or how long you have been walking with God, there is a storm out on the ocean headed your way. If you are not firmly anchored in Jesus you will surely drift into danger.

Who will you call on when the waves are crashing over your head? Hopefully, you already know a believer who has the mind of God and a passion to mend broken lives.

No Cliques!

When Paul writes, *"if a man is overtaken in any trespass* (Galatians 6:1), he is not talking about a close friend or someone you hang out with. The term "man" refers to *all mankind*—the human race—*any* person.

Those who have a mindset to restore others are not "a respecter of persons." As believers we cannot operate in cliques—with a special group over here and another over there. We are in the body *together*, which means "I am my brother's keeper."

Of course, there are certain people we connect with and with whom we enter into covenant relationship. Friends are a vital part of life, yet we must not retreat into an exclusive circle.

"Why Should I Care?"

Even if you have absolutely nothing in common

with a certain individual, your heart should be touched when you see the person fall out of fellowship with God. Never flaunt the attitude, "Why should I care? I don't really know them."

Every part of the body of Christ is valuable. As scriptures tells us, *"...indeed there are many members, yet one body. And the eye cannot say to the hand, 'I have no need of you'; nor again the head to the feet, 'I have no need of you.' No, much rather, those members of the body which seem to be weaker are necessary. And those members of the body which we think to be less honorable, on these we bestow greater honor"* (1 Corinthians 12:20-23).

THERE IS NO SUCH THING AS "SENIORITY" OR "SPECIAL PRIVILEGES" IN THE BODY OF CHRIST.

There is no such thing as "seniority" or "special privileges" in the body of Christ.

Total Equality

Jesus compared God's Kingdom to an estate manager who went out early one morning to hire men to labor in his vineyard. They agreed to work for a dollar a day.

A few hours later he saw other unemployed men in the town square and said to them, *"'You also go into the vineyard, and whatever is right I will give you.' So they went. Again he went out about the sixth and the ninth hour, and did likewise. And about the eleventh hour he went out and found others standing idle, and said to them, 'Why have you been standing here idle all day?' They said to him, 'Because no one hired us.' He said to them, 'You also go into the vineyard, and whatever is right you will receive'"* (Matthew 20:4-7).

When the day's work was finished, the owner of the vineyard told his steward to *"Call the laborers and give them their wages, beginning with the last to the first"* (v.8).

Those hired at the eleventh hour came and were each given a dollar—the same pay as those who were hired first. You can imagine the indignation of those who had worked all day. After hearing their complaint, the owner said, "Friend, I have done you no wrong. Didn't you agree to work for a dollar?" And he added, "Is it not lawful for me to do what I wish with my own money?"

The point Jesus was making is: *"the last will be first, and the first last"* (v.15).

Just because someone has been serving the Lord six months and you have been in the church sixty years matters little to God. He is going to reward a faithful heart.

Hope and Help

What about you? Are you willing to reach out to those in need—regardless of their status in the church or where they stand in relationship to the Lord?

Just as God extended His hand to man by sending His only Son to earth, your Heavenly Father expects you to offer hope and help to those who have fallen. You will both be lifted!

CHAPTER 4

WHY THROW A TEMPEST TANTRUM?

Can you imagine what it must have been like when Jesus arrived on the scene? People didn't quite know what to think of this Man from Galilee. When the crowds began to follow Him and miracles multiplied, His critics threw a fit!

- The day Jesus first preached at the synagogue in His hometown of Nazareth, those who heard Him *"were filled with wrath, and rose up and thrust Him out of the city; and they led Him to the brow of the hill on which their city was built, that they might throw Him down over the cliff"* (Luke 4:28-29).
- After healing a man on the Sabbath, the Pharisees *"were filled with rage, and discussed with one another what they might do to Jesus"* (Luke 6:11).

53

■ When the Son of God had the boldness to clear the temple of money changers and merchandisers, *" the scribes and chief priests...sought how they might destroy Him; for they feared Him, because all the people were astonished at His teaching"* (Mark 11:18).

Oh, This Generation!

Jesus was fully aware of the temper tantrums launched against Him and addressed the issues with this metaphor: *"But to what shall I liken this generation? It is like children sitting in the marketplaces and calling to their companions, and saying:*

> *'We played the flute for you,*
> *And you did not dance;*
> *We mourned to you,*
> *And you did not lament.'*

For John came neither eating nor drinking, and they say, 'He has a demon.' The Son of Man came eating and drinking, and they say, 'Look, a glutton and a winebibber, a friend of tax collectors and sinners!' But wisdom is justified by her children" (Matthew11:16-19).

Jesus was being charged with gluttony, drunkenness and having bad associations. At the same time, they thought John, the "forerunner" of the

Messiah, was absolutely crazy!

In essence, Jesus was saying, "You call the Baptist a madman because he fasts, while you want to have a feast. You attack me for eating with publicans, while you insist on strict separation from sinners. You despise the message of repentance and you loathe the proclamation of the Gospel. So you play your childish game with God's messenger while the world is headed for ruin."

Driving a Wedge

The judgment of John was harsh. Here was a man who came on the scene as a voice from the wilderness—who came walking in from the dessert. The Bible says he *"was clothed with camel's hair and with a leather belt around his waist, and he ate locusts and wild honey"* (Mark 1:6).

This is the same attire worn by Elijah and other prophets (2 Kings 1:8; Zechariah 13:4).

THE CRITICS WERE DETERMINED TO DRIVE A WEDGE BETWEEN JESUS AND JOHN.

The critics were determined to drive a wedge between Jesus and John, yet the Lord called their bluff, saying, "John kept himself untainted and didn't associate with sinners, but you wouldn't receive him. I come along with a more liberal approach, eating and drinking with everyone and you accuse me of not being religious enough."

There is only one conclusion we can come to: if people are looking for an excuse to criticize, they will always find one! In the words of the fault-finders, John was too tough and Jesus was too lax. They were especially offended because Jesus was a friend of the tax collectors—considered thieves since they worked for the Roman Empire and skimmed off extra money for themselves.

> **IF PEOPLE ARE LOOKING FOR AN EXCUSE TO CRITICIZE, THEY WILL ALWAYS FIND ONE!**

The Wrong Profile

Why did these people call John the Baptist a "demon"? Because he didn't hang out at the social club with a wine cooler or sit around and gossip after a prayer meeting. Instead, he represented order and structure and regulations people despised. His messages were stringent and too hard for their liking. Since they could not force him to bend his rules, he didn't fit their profile.

People never seem to change. They want commendation rather than condemnation, a pat on the back instead of a hickory stick. And they prefer no rules rather than God's law.

I'm glad the Lord never asked me to preach only what people "like" or what tickles their ears. He directed me to declare the truth—whether it is accepted or not. Jesus declared, *"And you shall know the truth, and the truth shall make you free"* (John 8:32).

In a church, certain rules are necessary:

- If you don't attend choir rehearsal, you don't sing on Sunday.
- If you don't pay your tithe, you can't become a deacon or elder.
- If you are not faithful in attendance, you can't be a leader.

"Playful Saints"

The point of tension in Matthew 11 comes when Jesus says the people are "like children"—mindless, immature, playful, contrary and hard to please.

Stop for a moment and you realize Jesus was also speaking to *our* generation. Today, people can have two loaves of bread under their arm and still be unhappy. Some say, "If God will give me a financial breakthrough I will serve Him until I die." Then, when they receive what they pray for, they may never darken the door of a church again.

As a pastor, I see "playful saints" who flirt with the devil—coming as close to the edge as possible. What they fail to realize is Satan doesn't play fair. Yes, he knows how to give you what makes you feel good, but when he lures you into his web, you're trapped.

"Old Fashioned?"

If Christ were physically walking the earth this very day, His message would not need to change. We live in a godless society where people have little reverence or fear for God. Atheists attempt to make us feel we are crazy and old fashioned in our belief. Even the liberal press mocks and ridicules believers. The situation was written about long ago by David: *"The fool has said in his heart, 'There is no God'"* (Psalm 14:1).

Our fashion, music, culture and world view is definitely not the same as it was 20 years ago. Even the church has changed to a more contemporary style of worship and message.

However, I am thankful that beneath the surface, there is still a body of believers governed by the principles of our apostolic fathers and *"Jesus Christ is the same yesterday, today, and forever"* (Hebrews 13:8).

Put Away Childish Things

Isn't it time we grow up?

The real difference between a man and a boy is the lessons learned. As children, we repeat the same mistakes—falling over hundreds of times before we learn to stand on our own two feet.

Men become men only when they learn from life's experiences. Your age or biological makeup doesn't automatically make you an adult. If you keep going around the same mountain you simply return to where you started. However, somewhere along the road you learn to make sound decisions—finally finding the route which will lead you to the crest of the mountain.

Paul writes, *"When I was a child, I spoke as a child, I understood as a child, I thought as a child; but when I became a man, I put away childish things"* (1 Corinthians 13:11).

Thank God, I don't make the same choices as when I was

> **IF YOU KEEP GOING AROUND THE SAME MOUNTAIN YOU SIMPLY RETURN TO WHERE YOU STARTED.**

young, playful and immature. There were certain traps I fell into when I lacked common sense. But when I grew up, those attractions no longer lured me.

The reason many teens and young adults have such a difficult time handling correction, even self-discipline, is because they cannot see the future. Many will be saddled by financial debt tomorrow with what they are squandering today. They are not mature enough to pay and enjoy at the same time.

Danger of Infection

If you don't take your Christian growth and development seriously you are playing Russian roulette with your future. I've met those with negative viruses who are highly contagious—and people who come too close will start having the same symptoms. Before long they look, talk and act like the one who is infected. Their frown produces your frown. When they lose their temper, so do you.

IF YOU DON'T TAKE YOUR CHRISTIAN GROWTH AND DEVELOPMENT SERIOUSLY YOU ARE PLAYING RUSSIAN ROULETTE WITH YOUR FUTURE.

I believe it is time we become filled with the love of the Savior—not consumed with buddies, pals, worldly friendships or people's opinion. Anyone who means so much to you that you have to imitate their behavior indicates something is wrong. Don't let anyone block the flow of God in your life.

When you come to Christ there must be such a transformation it shows in your physical appearance and behavior. You should start looking, talking and acting like Jesus.

A Cross to Carry

Many want religion, but since they are "childish" have no idea what they are searching for. They want to be "saved," yet don't understand salvation because they come from a "if it feels good, do it" generation.

Where did they learn the idea the road to heaven is easy? There is a cross to carry and a mountain to climb. The Bible tells us *"all who desire to live godly in Christ Jesus will suffer persecution"* (1 Timothy 3:12).

Yet, every trial and test will be worth the pain. In the words of Peter the disciple, *"Beloved, do not think it strange concerning the fiery trial which is to try you, as though some strange thing happened to you; but rejoice to the extent that you partake of Christ's sufferings, that when His glory is revealed, you may also be glad with exceeding joy"* (1 Peter 4:12-13).

An Act of Mercy

As a child, it is impossible to comprehend the sacrifice being made by parents. You don't know the rigors of standing eight hours a day on a job until your feet swell—just to put aside money for food, clothing, automobile insurance and college tuition.

Sons and daughters only begin to understand the investment of mom and dad when they start having families of their own. Until then you "play" with your parent's money, even abuse it.

Maturity also brings you to the realization your Heavenly Father paid a tremendous price for your salvation. He gave His only Son, Jesus, so you could have eternal life. It is an act of mercy we must not take lightly.

Concerning communion, the Bible says, *"But let a man examine himself, and so let him eat of the bread and drink of the cup. For he who eats and drinks in an unworthy manner eats and drinks judgment to himself, not discerning the Lord's body"* (1 Corinthians 11:28-29).

If we fail to examine ourselves, we may be crucifying the Lord afresh—saying His sacrifice and the propitiation for our sins is not worthy.

The Love Factor

When you become spiritually mature there is no longer room for hatred, strife, jealously or venting your anger. These are all replaced by divine love.

> **WHEN YOU BECOME SPIRITUALLY MATURE THERE IS NO LONGER ROOM FOR HATRED, STRIFE, JEALOUSY OR VENTING YOUR ANGER.**

In the words of the apostle Paul, *"Though I speak with the tongues of men and of angels, but have not love, I have become sounding brass or a clanging cymbal. And though I have the gift of prophecy, and understand all mysteries and all knowledge, and though I have all faith, so that I could remove mountains, but have not love, I am nothing. And though I bestow all my* goods to feed the poor, and though I give my body to be burned, but have not love, it profits me nothing" (1 Corinthians 13:1-3).

Without a demonstration of compassion, the song you sing to the world is one of discord.

Take a Deep Breath

If you are constantly looking for reasons to criticize and complain, you won't have to search too far—negativity will come running toward you.

Today, ask the Lord to replace bitterness and anger with His perfect peace. The next time you are about to lose your cool, take a deep breath and say, "Lord, I have given you my heart, now I am asking you to control my tongue."

Pray with the psalmist, *"Let the words of my mouth and the meditation of my heart be acceptable in Your sight, O Lord, my strength and my Redeemer"* (Psalm19:14).

You will then know what it means to feel a calming wave of God's awesome presence.

Chapter 5

The Menacing Clouds of Misunderstanding

Let me tell you about one of the largest auxiliary programs found in any church. It has the most members, the greatest influence and an incredible number of leaders. I call it "The Ministry of Misunderstanding."

If I've heard it once, I have heard it a hundred times: "Pastor, people just don't understand me!"

Try as we might, some individuals take our words and actions the wrong way. For example, Mary may be in a committee meeting where someone suggests a new outreach for the youth program and she responds, "Well, I'm going to have to pray about that."

Within a few hours the phones lines of gossip are humming with people saying, "Can you believe Mary is against expanding our youth program?"

All she wanted was more time to consider the proposal and now Mary has been cast as a roadblock. What caused the problem? Misinformation.

The Root Cause

I've seen the most innocent statements become like a small match igniting a huge prairie fire. Words taken out of context—or mistaken motives—can begin a destructive cycle that engulfs emotions and leads to a great divide.

Most church "splits" are the result of a minor issue blown beyond proportion.

I'm sure you know of relationships which have become permanently damaged because of a quarrel that spiraled out of control. Like the Hatfields and McCoys, some family feuds last for generations.

What causes misunderstandings? Here are just a few factors:

- Ignorance—not knowing all the facts.
- Pride—the inability to say "I was wrong."
- A "them and us" mentality—focusing on division rather than unity.
- Assumptions—presuming to know what you don't.
- Poor communication—not being able to articulate your idea or concept.

Troubled and Torn

Pardon me for being somewhat negative, but I've seen too many people in the church who are warped in their thinking. They don't seem to struggle with *overt* sins such as drinking, smoking or adultery. In fact, their outward lives seem as pure as the driven snow. Mentally, however, they seem troubled and torn—holding grudges against fellow believers and looking for every opportunity to tear down instead of build up.

What a tragedy to observe someone praying in a heavenly language, yet that same individual won't walk across the aisle to speak to their brother and sister in English.

"SOME OF YOU ARE SO SPIRITUAL YOU CANNOT IDENTIFY WITH THE STRUGGLES OF ANYONE ELSE."

There are men and women who say, "I am going to speak things that are not as though they were—and watch it come to pass." However, they don't know how to discern the pressure and pain of the person sitting in the pew right next to them.

As I tell my congregation, "Some of you are so spiritual you cannot identify with the struggles of anyone else."

A Covenant Relationship

Do we really understand what it means to be in covenant with God and His people? Or is that, too, a misunderstanding.

We say, "Because I am saved I am an heir of God and a joint heir with Christ—and everything that belongs to the Lord belongs to me."

There is a far greater meaning to *covenant* than just being an heir to possessions. It is also an agreement between you and me—in spite of aspects of my behavior or personality you don't like. Because we are in a divine relationship, you do not have to compromise with my weaknesses, yet you love me at all times.

Why don't we see this practiced in the church?

Instead, we have the kind of covenant which says, "When Brother Jones doesn't act the way I think he should, I do not want to be bothered with him anymore."

With such a spirit of pride, jealousy and condemnation, how can we expect a move of God? Remember, the Lord does not operate in a climate of confusion.

Ego-Driven?

Pay attention to what Paul writes to the believers in Galatia: *"Bear one another's burdens, and so fulfill the law of Christ. For if anyone thinks himself to be something, when he is nothing, he deceives himself"* (Galatians 6:2-3).

As I told a friend, "I've come across people who think they are the chips, the dips and the movie!"

Some ego-driven folks think the world should pay them homage because they own tailor made clothes, luxury cars and a blue chip stock portfolio.

Such individuals not only misunderstand life, they have no concept of what is pleasing to the Almighty. God is looking for those who look at their heart and say, "I was a filthy rag and did not deserve to be

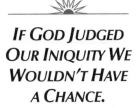

IF GOD JUDGED OUR INIQUITY WE WOULDN'T HAVE A CHANCE.

forgiven, but the Lord looked past my faults and saw my need."

If God judged our iniquity we wouldn't have a chance. However, He saves us in spite of ourselves.

Train to Manhattan

When it comes to pride, I speak from experience.

After graduating from Fairleigh Dickinson University with a degree in mass media communications, I moved to California where I worked for four years as an electrical engineer—installing main frame telephone equipment.

This wasn't exactly my cup of tea, so after four years I returned to the east coast and landed a job in New York City at Savoy Records as the National Director of Promotions. The title was better than the pay, but I was really excited about being in the music business.

I took the train every morning into midtown Manhattan.

The Christmas Party

One day, as I walked into the office, the president of the company stopped me and asked, "Is that your napsack?"

"DON'T YOU KNOW WHO YOU ARE?"

"Yes sir, it is," I responded.

"Don't you know who you are?" the president replied indignantly. "You can't be coming into this office as the National Director of Promotions with a napsack!"

Trying to laugh it off, I said, "Well, if you think I need a briefcase, perhaps you need to buy one for me." And we dropped the topic.

Time went by and we were having a Christmas party at the office—one where "grab bag" gifts were exchanged.

When I opened mine, I was absolutely stunned.

Here was a beautiful leather Louis Vuitton briefcase. I thought to myself, "Wow! God is good!"

The Strap Broke!

You have no idea how proud I was of that case. Every morning on the train, I'd swing it back and forth—just to make sure people could get a good look.

It had straps on the side and one to put over your shoulder. Unfortunately, I had the case only a few weeks when suddenly one of the straps broke.

Immediately, I found a phone book and located the address of the Louis Vuitton store on Fifth Avenue. Then, marching in like I owned the place, I took the case, threw it on the counter and said to the refined saleslady, "I know my boss paid a lot for this. So why would the strap break on a Louis Vuitton briefcase?"

In a soft voice, the woman said, "Calm down, sir. We have customers."

"I'm not calming down," I retorted. "I want this repaired."

"Of course," she reassured me. "We'll handle it."

The well-dressed woman put her glasses on, carefully examined the case, and commented, "Sir...."

"Yes," I replied anxiously.

"Sir, we don't repair imitation Louis Vuittons."

Embarrassed beyond words, I sheepishly backed out of the store. I had been walking around Manhattan flaunting a fake Louis Vuitton and didn't even know it. No wonder the strap broke!

"Imitation" Believers

Perhaps you have encountered people in the church who are the same. When pressure enters their lives, their spiritual straps snap and they wonder why. Could it be because they are fake Christians?

Individuals such as these are not anointed and have no faith because they are "imitation" believers.

Let's stop deceiving ourselves and come to an altar of repentance and ask the Lord to place within us a new heart and a genuine spirit.

Blocking a Blessing

Some people question, "I go to church. Why isn't my life being blessed? Or, "I try to read my Bible every day. Why don't I have joy and peace?"

If this is you, perhaps you need to take an inventory of your relationships with fellow believers. How many have you harmed through spreading gossip or bearing rumors? Is there someone for whom you hold bitterness or anger? Who do you need to approach and ask, "Will you forgive me?"

Since God is willing and waiting to pour out a blessing on your life, don't allow anything to close the windows of heaven.

Twisting Words

Being a pastor, one of the most delicate moments of ministry is when I feel led to privately correct a church member for some action or behavior I feel is harming both the individual and the work of God

I am always aware that how the individual talks about the encounter has the potential for great misunderstanding. More than once, a believer who knows absolutely nothing about the situation becomes upset with me for attempting to lift a fellow Christian to a higher level of excellence.

At times I feel like the psalmist, who writes: *"All day they twist my words; all their thoughts are against me for evil"* (Psalm 56:5).

CORRECTION IN THE CHURCH IS NOT PERSONAL, IT IS BUSINESS— GOD'S BUSINESS!

In reality, correction in the church is not personal, it is business—*God's* business!

Sharp Contention

Even among the best of friends, misunderstandings can cause setbacks and division.

Paul and Barnabas were quite a team—blazing a missionary trail for the cause of Christ. They preached together at Antioch, on the island of Cyprus, at Iconium, Listra and Derbe and even before the council at Jerusalem.

At one point on their journey Paul said to Barnabas, *"Let us now go back and visit our brethren in every city where we have preached the word of the Lord, and see how they are doing"* (Acts 15:36).

Barnabas was determined to take John along—the one nicknamed Mark. But Paul wouldn't hear of it because he thought Mark was a quitter and had jumped ship on them in Pamphylia.

As scripture records, *"Then the contention became so sharp that they parted from one another"* (v.39).

So Barnabas took Mark and sailed to Cyprus, but Paul chose Silas and departed for Syria and Cilicia to strengthen the work of Christ there.

The disagreement wasn't permanent. Later, in his letter to the believers at Corinth, Paul commends Barnabas as a noble example of ministry (1 Corinthians 9:6). What about Mark? Paul eventually grew to admire him so much he requested that he be with him during his final days (2 Timothy 4:11).

Mercy and Pardon

How did Jesus deal with those who misunderstood Him? In His Sermon on the Mount He said, *"...love your enemies, bless those who curse you, do good to those who hate you, and pray for those who spitefully use you and persecute you, that you may be sons of your Father in heaven; for He makes His sun rise on the evil and on the good, and sends rain on the just and on the unjust"* (Matthew 5:44-45).

Later, during His darkest hours, when He was about to be put to death, Jesus demonstrated mercy and pardon. Scripture records, *"And when they had come to the place called Calvary, there they crucified Him, and the criminals, one on the right hand and the other on the left. Then Jesus said, 'Father, forgive them, for they do not know what they do'"* (Luke 23:32-24).

The High Road

Why allow a small gust of wind to become a dangerous tornado? That's what will happen if you don't nip misunderstanding in the bud.

The moment you have the first inkling your words or actions are being misconstrued, address the issue before it has a chance to cause damage. And, if you are on the receiving end of rumor or misinformation, take the high road. Be quick to forgive and have a short memory regarding the offense.

"Do not be overcome by evil, but overcome evil with good" (Romans 12:21).

Will you start demonstrating this sound advice?

CHAPTER 6

"LORD, SEND A GUST OF WIND!"

Do you remember when you were a kid and your mom or dad took you into an open field with a brand new kite? You could hardly wait to see it soaring above your head.

However, if it was a calm day, no matter how fast you ran with the string clenched in your hand, the kite wouldn't lift off the ground. Why? Because it takes a breeze—wind pressure—to make the kite fly.

Sure, we would all like to sail through life without encountering a storm, but God prepares us for tough times step by step, starting with a gentle breeze. If we can handle it, He takes us to the next step, and the next. Finally, we are ready to face anything that may come our way.

Steps to Courage

I'm sure you recall the story of David and Goliath.

How did this young man have the courage to take on a giant—the mighty Philistine?

If you read the account, David developed his courage in stages—starting with what was easy, then tackling what was more difficult. When he first comes on the scene, this shepherd boy was chosen to be in the service of King Saul because David could play the harp. The Bible say, *"...whenever the spirit from God was upon Saul, David would take a harp and play it with his hand. Then Saul would become refreshed"* (1 Samuel 16:23).

DAVID DEVELOPED HIS COURAGE IN STAGES—STARTING WITH WHAT WAS EASY, THEN TACKLING WHAT WAS MORE DIFFICULT.

A Giant Challenge

Next, we learn that Saul favored David so much he made him one of his armor bearers.

Then came the threat to Israel from the Philistines. The two armies were facing each other, ready for a showdown, when their champion, Goliath, stepped forward to make a challenge. This 9-feet tall giant, dressed in full battle gear, shouted in a loud voice, *"Choose a man for yourselves, and let him come down to me. If he is able to fight with me and kill me, then we will be your servants. But if I prevail against him and kill him, then you shall be our servants and serve us"* (1 Samuel 17:8-9).

Saul and his armies were terrified. For the next 40 days the same challenge was issued, yet not one Israelite could be found to fight Goliath, even though Saul offered a great reward. He announced, *"...and it shall be that the man who kills him the king will enrich with great riches, will give him his daughter, and give his father's house exemption from taxes in Israel"* (v.25).

Wow! That was quite an offer!

"Inch by Inch"

To the surprise of everyone, "little "David stepped forward and informed the king, *"Let no man's heart fail because of him; your servant will go and fight with this Philistine"* (v.32).

Saul was stunned, and said to David, *"You are not able to go against this Philistine to fight with him; for you are a youth, and he a man of war from his youth"* (v.33).

DAVID DIDN'T START BY TACKLING A GIANT, FIRST THERE WAS A LION AND A BEAR.

David surprised Saul by telling how he had faced earlier encounters and was ready for the ultimate battle.

He told the king, *"Your servant used to keep his father's sheep, and when a lion or a bear came and took a lamb out of the flock, I went out after it and struck it, and delivered the lamb from its mouth; and when it arose against me, I caught it by its beard, and*

79

struck and killed it. Your servant has killed both lion and bear; and this uncircumcised Philistine will be like one of them, seeing he has defied the armies of the living God"(vv.34-36). And he added, *"The Lord who delivered me from the paw of the lion and from the paw of the bear, He will deliver me from the hand of this Philistine"* (v.37).

It's been said, "Inch by inch it's a cinch." David didn't start by tackling a giant, first there was a lion and a bear. With this kind of confidence under his belt he was able to kill Goliath with just a slingshot and five smooth stones.

A Prelude for Victory

Today, you may be confronting the greatest crisis you have ever encountered—so threatening you question, "How am I ever going to make it through."

Let me tell you how. Pause for as long as it takes to reflect on the problems you faced five, ten or fifteen years ago. They may seem insignificant in comparison, but those difficulties came into your life for a reason. Just as a child crawls before he walks and walks before he runs, God has prepared you for this day,

Every small skirmish is a prelude for a larger victory. This is why you can say, "If I made it then, with God's help I can make it now!"

"Light" Affliction?

Paul, the apostle, had an amazing attitude. To the believers at Corinth he wrote, *"For our light affliction, which is but for a moment, is working for us a far more exceeding and eternal weight of glory"* (2 Corinthians 4:17).

Most of us would react, "Affliction is affliction—and it's all bad!"

Paul, however, had a different view. He realized that every problem in life is "light" when you consider the alternative. Since light is the opposite of heavy, the apostle was right when he compared life's temporary problems to an eternal "weight" of glory.

Listen to what Paul refers to as minor complaints. He writes, *"From the Jews five times I received forty stripes minus one. Three times I was beaten with rods; once I was stoned; three times I was shipwrecked; a night and a day I have been in the deep; in journeys often, in perils of waters, in perils of robbers, in perils of my own countrymen, in perils of the Gentiles, in perils in the city, in perils in the wilderness, in perils in the sea, in perils among false brethren; in weariness and toil, in sleeplessness often, in hunger and thirst, in fastings often, in cold and nakedness"* (2 Corinthians 11:24-27).

If just one of those calamities came our way we would be bawling our eyes out and pleading for help. Paul, however, was not complaining; he was just stating the facts.

To him, these were passing perils. The pain and suffering he experienced was nothing compared with the joy he had in serving Jesus—and the eternity with Christ waiting ahead.

Strength in Weakness

Later, when Paul had a thorn in the flesh, the Lord spoke to him, saying, *"My grace is sufficient for you, for My strength is made perfect in weakness"* (2 Corinthians 12:9).

Through all of this, Paul could rejoice, *"Therefore most gladly I will rather boast in my infirmities, that the power of Christ may rest upon me. Therefore I take pleasure in infirmities, in reproaches, in needs, in persecutions, in distresses, for Christ's sake. For when I am weak, then I am strong"* (2 Corinthians 12:9-10).

It would be a good idea to write these verses on a card and tape it to your refrigerator door. Commit the words to memory—then every time you start complaining about a test or trial ask God to forgive you. Look up to heaven and say, "Thank You, Lord, for this problem. I know it is helping me to grow stronger in You!"

A New Perspective

If you have accepted Christ as your Lord and

Savior, it's time to eliminate the negative "woe is me" language from your vocabulary. Your problems are minor in the light of eternity—and it's time to see them from a new perspective.

Jesus says, *"Take My yoke upon you and learn from Me, for I am gentle and lowly in heart, and you will find rest for your souls. For My yoke is easy and My burden is light"* (Matthew 11:29-30).

What a difference it makes when we replace the heavy constraints of sin with the yoke of Christ. The reason His burden is *light* is because it brings freedom, liberty and release. Suddenly, you are free!

> **WHAT A DIFFERENCE IT MAKES WHEN WE REPLACE THE HEAVY CONSTRAINTS OF SIN WITH THE YOKE OF CHRIST.**

Thank God, we do not have to suffer the weight of the cross. At Calvary, Christ became our substitute. The thorns were pressed into *His* brow, the spears were thrust into *His* side and the nails were driven into *His* hands.

Again, by comparison, our afflictions are light.

Seeing the Kingdom

The most necessary gust of wind you will ever receive is the one which results in your personal salvation.

83

When a Pharisee named Nicodemus came to Jesus at night, flattering Him by saying, *"Rabbi, we know that You are a teacher come from God; for no one can do these signs that You do unless God is with him"* (John 3:2).

Jesus looked at this member of the Jewish ruling counsel and got right to the point. He said, *"Most assuredly, I say to you, unless one is born again, he cannot see the kingdom of God"* (v.3).

"The Wind Blows"

Born again? This was a brand new concept to Nicodemus. He asked, *"How can a man be born when he is old? Can he enter a second time into his mother's womb and be born?"* (v.4).

Jesus answered, *"...unless one is born of water and the Spirit, he cannot enter the kingdom of God. That which is born of the flesh is flesh, and that which is born of the Spirit is spirit. Do not marvel that I said to you, 'You must be born again'"* (vv.5-7).

Then Jesus typified salvation as a wind. He told Nicodemus, *"The wind blows where it wishes, and you hear the sound of it, but cannot tell where it comes from and where it goes. So is everyone who is born of the Spirit"* (v.8).

It was during this same encounter Jesus uttered these powerful, life-changing words: *"For God so loved the world that He gave His only begotten Son, that whoever believes in Him should not perish but have everlasting life"* (v.16).

The "Second Wind"

If you ever talk with a marathon runner, they'll tell you how, after running several miles, they suddenly get their "second wind."

Well, as a child of God, you can know this too. Just as the born again experience is like a heavenly breeze, the Father has something more powerful in store for you—the Holy Spirit. This "second wind" is described as "rushing" and "mighty!"

Just before Jesus was taken up into heaven, He told His followers, *"not to depart from Jerusalem, but to wait for the Promise of the Father, which...you have heard from* **THIS "SECOND WIND" IS DESCRIBED AS "RUSHING" AND "MIGHTY!"** *Me; for John truly baptized with water, but you shall be baptized with the Holy Spirit not many days from now"* (Acts 1:4-5).

It happened! On the day of Pentecost, 120 were gathered in the Upper Room in earnest prayer when *"suddenly there came a sound from heaven, as of a rushing mighty wind, and it filled the whole house where they were sitting"* (Acts 2:2).

The Holy Spirit descended in power.

What a God we serve! He gives us His best—then keeps heaping blessing upon blessing.

The Stages of Faith

I've meet many men and women in the Kingdom who have tremendous faith. Yet, most will agree they didn't begin that way. The Bible says *"God has dealt to each one a measure of faith"* (Romans 12:3). This is our starting point—and we all have an equal amount.

There was a time when the disciples had *little* faith. During a great storm on Galilee, with waves sweeping over the boat, they woke Jesus, pleading "Save us. We're going to drown."

He replied, *"Why are you fearful, O you of little faith?"* (Matthew 8:26). Then Jesus arose and rebuked the winds and the sea, and there was a great calm.

Your faith doesn't need to remain small. The Bible records, *"Stephen, full of faith and power, did great wonders and signs among the people"* (Acts 6:8).

There are those with a *measure* of faith, *little* faith, *full* of faith, and there is also *great* faith. To the centurion who asked Jesus to just "say the word" so that his servant would be healed, the Lord declared, *"I have not found so great faith, no, not in Israel"* (Luke 7:9).

What kind of faith is yours?

Learning to Fly

How can we grow strong if there is nothing shaping our character. How can we believe for more if there is nothing to stretch our faith? How can we fly if there is nothing beneath our wings?

Perhaps we need to pray, "Lord, send a gust of wind."

CHAPTER 7

HOW SAFE IS YOUR SHELTER?

The construction business isn't for amateurs.

You can build the most up-to-date, architecturally detailed home in the world, but unless you have taken the time to dig a strong, solid foundation, eventually the walls will begin to crack and you'll be in for some enormous repair bills!

This problem has always persisted. Jesus made the point in this parable: *"Whoever comes to Me, and hears My sayings and does them, I will show you whom he is like: He is like a man building a house, who dug deep and laid the foundation on the rock. And when the flood arose, the stream beat vehemently against that house, and could not shake it, for it was founded on the rock. But he who heard and did nothing is like a man who built a house on the earth without a foundation, against which the stream beat vehemently; and immediately it fell. And the ruin of that house was great"* (Luke 6:47-49).

It is only by faithfully *following* Christ and obeying the Word, we can find the Rock on which to construct a "strong house" that will last for eternity—*"...a place of refuge, and for a shelter from storm and rain"* (Isaiah 4:6).

Here are three benefits of building on God's foundation:

- **You'll find salvation.** *"Truly my soul silently waits for God; from Him comes my salvation. He only is my rock and my salvation; He is my defense; I shall not be greatly moved"* (Psalm 62:1-2).
- **You'll find deliverance**. *"The Lord is my rock and my fortress and my deliverer; My God, my strength, in whom I will trust; My shield and the horn of my salvation, my stronghold"* (Psalm 18:2).
- **You'll find protection**. *"For You have been a shelter for me, a strong tower from the enemy"* (Psalm 61:3).

Envy, Strife, Division

One of the great lessons found in the Bible on building a strong spiritual foundation was written by

Paul to the members of the church at Corinth. It is obvious he was totally frustrated with the unspiritual way the believers were dealing with each other.

Paul scolds them, saying, *"And I, brethren, could not speak to you as to spiritual people but as to carnal, as to babes in Christ. I fed you with milk and not with solid food; for until now you were not able to receive it, and even now you are still not able; for you are still carnal. For where there are envy, strife, and divisions among you, are you not carnal and behaving like mere men?* (1 Corinthians 3:1-3).

The Futility of Following Man

The problem was, the people were taking sides between listening to Paul (the evangelist) or Apollos—a teacher who worked in the established church, edifying the converts Paul had won to Christ.

IT IS ALWAYS FUTILE TO BLINDLY FOLLOW MAN.

The believers were acting like children—causing upheaval and discord for no good reason. The apostle told them, *"For when one says, 'I am of Paul,' and another, 'I am of Apollos,' are you not carnal?"* (v.4).

It is always futile to blindly follow man. Everything you are is because of the grace and mercy of Jesus—including your ability to think and function.

It's His *favor* which gives you joy unspeakable and fills you with glory.

The Lord gives each one of us special gifts. Yours is no greater than mine and what He gives to an evangelist is not superior to what is given to a pastor or teacher.

As the apostle explains, *"Who then is Paul, and who is Apollos, but ministers through whom you believed, as the Lord gave to each one? I planted, Apollos watered, but God gave the increase. So then neither he who plants is anything, nor he who waters, but God who gives the increase. Now he who plants and he who waters are one, and each one will receive his own reward according to his own labor* (vv.5-8).

Who gives the increase? Jehovah! A variety of individuals can contribute to your life, but never look to them as your ultimate source. Only Almighty God can multiply your seed.

Sowing in a Famine?

Our Heavenly Father's economy is totally different from man's. For example, when Abraham died the people were facing starvation due to a great famine in the land (Genesis 26:1). Because of the drought, the hungry people were fleeing to Egypt.

However, here's what the Lord told Abraham's son, Isaac: *"Do not go down to Egypt; live in the land of which I shall tell you. Dwell in this land, and I will be with you and bless you; for to you and your descendants I give all these lands, and I will perform the oath which I swore to Abraham your father"* (vv.2-3).

At a time when crops were failing and people were starving, he took the last remaining seed he owned and, by faith, placed it in the parched, arid ground. The Bible says, *"Then Isaac sowed in that land"* (v.12).

If he had been swayed by the masses, Isaac would have abandoned the field and taken the next camel to Cairo! But God spoke and Isaac *"reaped in the same year a hundredfold; and the Lord blessed him* (v.12).

This was just the starting point of Isaac's bountiful harvest. The Bible records, *"The man began to prosper, and continued...until he became very prosperous; for he had possessions of flocks and possessions of herds and a great number of servants. So the Philistines envied him"* (vv.13-14).

IT IS THE GIVER, NOT THE RECEIVER, WHO PROVIDES PROSPERITY AND INCREASE.

It is the Giver, not the receiver, who provides prosperity and increase.

You are "God's Building"

This is the same lesson Paul was trying to get through the stubborn heads of the quarreling believers at Corinth! He told them: *"For we are God's fellow workers; you are God's field, you are God's building"* (1 Corinthians 3:9).

If we are truly Christians, when people look at us they should see a representative of the Lord. Those who are divisive or deceitful need to ask themselves, "Why would I want to disgrace my Father and make Him look so bad?"

THE BEDROCK FOUNDATION OF YOUR LIFE MUST BE CHRIST—NOT YOU, NOR ANOTHER MAN OR WOMAN.

The bedrock foundation of your life must be Christ—not you, nor another man or woman.

Paul writes: *"According to the grace of God which was given to me, as a wise master builder I have laid the foundation, and another builds on it. But let each one take heed how he builds on it. For no other foundation can anyone lay than that which is laid, which is Jesus Christ. Now if anyone builds on this foundation with gold, silver, precious stones, wood, hay, straw, each one's work will become clear; for the Day will declare it, because it will be revealed by fire; and the fire will test each one's work, of what sort it is. If anyone's work which he has built on it endures, he will receive a reward"* (vv.10-14).

The Lord is the foundation, but you have been

94

commissioned as the house *builder*. What kind of material will you use? Will you use inferior materials which will one day burn, or stones which will last for eternity?

What a Mansion!

Most people never think about the fact that the quality of the spiritual house you build on earth will determine the kind of home God is preparing for you in heaven. I am expecting a *"full reward"* (2 John 1:8)—and pray you are, too!

Jesus talked about the dwelling place He is getting ready for His children. *"Let not your heart be troubled; you believe in God, believe also in Me. In My Father's house are many mansions; if it were not so, I would have told you. I go to prepare a place for you. And if I go and prepare a place for you, I will come again and receive you to Myself; that where I am, there you may be also"* (John 14:1-3).

What a marvelous promise! The same Christ who saved you is now in heaven waiting for you to join Him—in a city beyond description. It's amazing what John saw in his revelation: *"The construction of its wall was of jasper...the foundations of the wall of the city were adorned with all kinds of precious stones...And the street of the city was pure gold, like transparent glass"* (Revelation 21:18-21).

The city needed no sun or moon to shine, *"for the glory of God illuminated it. The Lamb is its light"* (v.23).

Best of all, the storms and trials we face on earth will all be distant history. *"And God will wipe away every tear from their eyes; there shall be no more death, nor sorrow, nor crying. There shall be no more pain, for the former things have passed away"* (Revelation 21:4).

What a glorious day that will be!

Only One Rock!

Earlier, when Jesus was describing the home He was preparing, Thomas, the doubter, asked, *"Lord, we do not know where You are going, and how can we know the way?"* John 14:5).

Jesus answered with the most authoritative words found in scripture: *"I am the way, the truth, and the life. No one comes to the Father except through Me"* (v.6).

Friend, you don't have to wait for heaven to have a safe, secure dwelling place. You can start building your life on a firm foundation today. The Son of God is not "a" way but *"the"* way—there is no other road to salvation.

Jesus is *"a living stone, rejected indeed by men, but chosen by God and precious"* (1 Peter 2:4). But there is more: *"...you also, as living stones, are being built up a spiritual house, a holy priesthood, to offer up spiritual sacrifices acceptable to God through Jesus Christ"* (1 Peter 2:4-5).

The Lord lives! Blessed be your Rock. Let the God of your salvation be exalted!

CHAPTER 8

DELIVERANCE FROM DISTRESS!

The moment you are *saved* you should accept your *deliverance*—since both terms mean you are set free!

The problem most people have is that they believe, yet they don't behave. The primary reason being they refuse to embrace correction.

In the Old Testament, salvation and chastisement were often linked together. For example, Solomon wrote: *"Do not withhold correction from a child, for if you beat him with a rod, he will not die. You shall beat him with a rod, and deliver his soul from hell"* (Proverbs 23:13-14).

Of course, the person who is administering the discipline must love the individual enough to see them delivered—they don't want the child to be forever lost.

Saved from Death

The same connection between salvation and deliverance is found in the story of the Israelites plea for David to return as king—after the disastrous reign of his son, Absalom. The Bible records, *"Now all the people were in a dispute throughout all the tribes of Israel, saying, 'The king saved us from the hand of our enemies, he delivered us from the hand of the Philistines, and now he has fled from the land because of Absalom'"* (2 Samuel 19:9).

As believers today, by proclaiming we are "saved," we are announcing we have been set free from those things that would cause our total destruction. God's Word declares:

- *"...he who turns a sinner from the error of his way will save a soul from death"* (James 5:19-20).
- *"For the law of the Spirit of life in Christ Jesus has made me free from the law of sin and death"* (Romans 8:2).
- *"For the wages of sin is death, but the gift of God is eternal life in Christ Jesus our Lord"* (Romans 6:12).

Since you are now saved, you should also be delivered from those things which would end your life.

Drinking, smoking, drugs and immoral behavior need to be placed at the foot of the Cross.

If there are aspects of your life which still need to be purged from the desires of the flesh, ask the Lord to sanctify you—starting today!

Set Free!

When you are walking in the Spirit you cannot simultaneously walk in the lusts of the flesh. If you are truly living for the Lord, the "bondage" of sin is broken. As Paul explains, *"...when we were children, were in bondage under the elements of the world. But when the fullness of the time had come, God sent forth His Son, born of a woman, born under the law, to redeem those who were under the law, that we might receive the adoption as sons. And because you are sons, God has sent forth the Spirit of His Son into your hearts, crying out, 'Abba, Father!' Therefore you are no longer a slave but a son, and if a son, then an heir of God through Christ"* (Galatians 4:3-7).

> **WHEN YOU ARE WALKING IN THE SPIRIT YOU CANNOT SIMULTANEOUSLY WALK IN THE LUSTS OF THE FLESH.**

Praise God! You have been miraculously saved— set free and delivered through Jesus!

The Turn-Around

The danger of slipping back into our old ways carries eternal danger. As the Word tells us, *"For if I build again those things which I destroyed, I make myself a transgressor"* (Galatians 2:18).

To repent means to turn around. So, when you are born again you stop doing what is wrong.

The reason people regress and fall back into sin is because they don't know how to walk away from what pleases the flesh.

- If certain movies cause you to be carnal, don't buy a ticket or rent the DVD.
- If gossip on the telephone is one of your problems, click the "end call" button.
- If hanging out with your girlfriend or boyfriend leads to immoral behavior, stop the relationship.
- Don't cut down to two packs of cigarettes a day. Throw the entire carton in the trash can once and for all!

Accept the fact you now have help in making these life-changing decisions. Christ is dwelling inside you. As Paul so wonderfully explains, *"I have been crucified with Christ; it is no longer I who live, but*

Christ lives in me; and the life which I now live in the flesh I live by faith in the Son of God, who loved me and gave Himself for me. I do not set aside the grace of God; for if righteousness comes through the law, then Christ died in vain" (Galatians 2:20-21).

When you see me, you are seeing God's Son. I am flesh, but Christ is Spirit.

Since we have an advocate with the Father, we nullify grace when we protest, "I cannot live a *delivered* life."

What's Your Role?

I've heard more than one individual use the excuse, "If God had wanted to deliver me from this habit, I'm sure He would have already done it!"

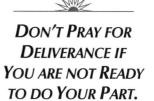

DON'T PRAY FOR DELIVERANCE IF YOU ARE NOT READY TO DO YOUR PART.

Friend, don't pray for deliverance if you are not ready to do your part. Faith without works is dead—this means you have an obligation for action. Paul says, *"this one thing I do"* (Phillip 3:13 KJV).

One of the great chapters on personal responsibility is James 1. He writes: *"Blessed is the man who endures temptation; for when he has been approved, he will receive the crown of life which the Lord has promised to those who love Him. Let no one say when he is tempted, 'I am tempted by God'; for God cannot be tempted by evil, nor does He Himself tempt anyone. But each one is tempted when he is drawn away by his own desires and enticed. Then, when desire has conceived, it gives birth to sin; and sin, when it is full-grown, brings forth death"* (James 1:12-15).

WHO ENDURES TEMPTATION? YOU DO!

Who endures temptation? You do!

Keep reading and you'll learn the danger of *pretending* you are a listener—letting the Word go in one ear and out the other. We are to *" be doers of the word, and not hearers only, deceiving yourselves. For if anyone is a hearer of the word and not a doer, he is like a man observing his natural face in a mirror; for he observes himself, goes away, and immediately forgets what kind of man he was. But he who looks into the perfect law of liberty and continues in it, and is not a forgetful hearer but a doer of the work, this one will be blessed in what he does"* (vv.22-25).

Deliverance is a united effort; we both have to do our part.

The Sorcerer

During the first wave of the spreading of the Gospel

after Jesus' return to heaven, Philip went to the city of Samaria to preach Christ and multitudes were saved, healed and delivered. The Bible records: *"...unclean spirits, crying with a loud voice, came out of many who were possessed; and many who were paralyzed and lame were healed. And there was great joy in that city"* (Acts 8:7-8).

However, there was a man in Samaria named Simon who had practiced sorcery for many years—and had most of the citizens saying, *"This man is the great power of God"* (v.10).

To the surprise of many, this sorcerer also embraced what was happening and *"continued with Philip, and was amazed, seeing the miracles and signs which were done"* (v.13).

The Priceless Gift

Word of the great revival reached the apostles who were in Jerusalem and they sent Peter and John to join Phillip. They prayed for the converts that they might receive the Holy Spirit, *"For as yet He had fallen upon none of them. They had only been baptized in the name of the Lord Jesus. Then they laid hands on them, and they received the Holy Spirit"* (vv.16-17).

When Simon saw that through the laying on of the apostles' hands the Holy Spirit was given, he offered them money, saying, *"Give me this power also, that anyone on whom I lay hands may receive the Holy Spirit"* (v.19).

Peter was outraged and retorted: *"Your money perish with you, because you thought that the gift of God could be purchased with money! You have neither part nor portion in this matter, for your heart is not right in the sight of God. Repent therefore of this your wickedness, and pray God if perhaps the thought of your heart may be forgiven you. For I see that you are poisoned by bitterness and bound by iniquity"* (vv.20-23).

Only then did Simon ask the apostles to pray for personal deliverance from these things.

A Spirit of Manipulation

Without question there are people who call themselves "born again" but have the mantle of a sorcerer on them. Let me explain. The word "witchcraft" derives from an old English word which means using sorcery or magic to manipulate a person's will.

Any person in the church who controls an outcome using their own devious plan is operating in the spirit of witchcraft. I even include pastors who keep congregations isolated from biblical truth—but constantly hammer their own ideology or twisted interpretation of scripture.

Beware of those who say, "Trust me. You don't have to search the Bible because I have done it for you."

Such a minister has perverted his authority. Good leadership does not design messages to coerce or control you, but to inform and give practical applications to use—so you can see it works. Then he tells you where you can find truth in scripture for yourself.

WHEN YOU LISTEN TO ONLY ONE VOICE, YOU ARE LOSING CONTROL OF YOUR WILL.

When you listen to only one voice, you are losing control of your will.

You were created as a free moral agent with the power to choose. Adam was not a robot; he could have listened to God instead of Eve. You should never be *made* to do anything—you have a say in the matter.

Examine Your Heart

Some try to deliver others when they have not been delivered themselves. As a result, what they attempt to accomplish boomerangs.

If you want to know what happens when the wrong person touches the things of God, read the story of

David and the Ark of the Lord.

After David defeated the Philistines and had been anointed king over Israel, he gathered 30,000 of his choice men to bring the precious Ark from Judah to Jerusalem. Scripture tells us they set it on a brand new cart and began their journey from the home of Adinadab, where it had been stored. On the way, *"David and all the house of Israel played music before the Lord on all kinds of instruments of fir wood, on harps, on stringed instruments, on tambourines...and on cymbals"* (2 Samuel 6:5).

Then, stopping at a threshing floor, an oxen pulling the cart stumbled and Uzzah, one of Adinadab's sons reached out and took hold of the Ark. This violated clear instructions on how the Ark was to be handled (Exodus 25): *"Then the anger of the Lord was aroused against Uzzah, and God struck him there for his error; and he died there by the ark of God"* (2 Samuel 6:7).

When you try to touch what is anointed without authority, you're playing with fire.

Immediately, David had the Ark of the Lord taken to the house of Obed-Edom—where it remained for three months. This was a man who knew how to respect God's presence and the Lord blessed him and his entire household (v.11).

A Buried Past!

Your deliverance begins with salvation—and continues as you walk in the Spirit, not the flesh.

Why turn back to the control and bondage of sin? If you made the decision to accept Christ, your are declaring, "Hallelujah, my past is gone! It is buried!"

Jesus came to heal the brokenhearted and *"to set at liberty those who are oppressed"* (Luke 4:18).

Start rejoicing and living in His freedom!

CHAPTER 9

FROM TURMOIL TO TRUST

Let's be honest. Most of the "messes" in our lives are of our own making. We ignore the warning signs and race full-throttle into hazardous territory and risky behavior.

We fail to hear the voice inside which tells us, "Stop! Danger ahead!" As a result, we are swamped by a rising tide of turmoil.

Who is to blame for our predicament? We are!

If you and I received what we deserved, we would experience severe punishment on earth and be denied eternity in heaven. Our future would be a "sentence of shame" rather than an offer of pardon.

"Not Guilty!"

Thank God, we have been given the chance to be

forgiven of our failings and ransomed from the web of sin in which we find ourselves. Instead of being convicted, we are declared "not guilty!"

What gives us the option to live a life of freedom? It is found in one word: *trust.* Because we have total faith and confidence that Christ's death on the Cross paid the penalty for our sin, we can confess our transgressions and know His blood cleanses our heart and wipes the slate clean.

The Bible tells us, *"The Lord redeems the soul of His servants, and none of those who trust in Him shall be condemned"* (Psalm 34:22).

"Paid in Full"

Think of it! If we place our complete faith in the Lord there is absolutely no sentence handed down for the iniquity of our past.

This is why Paul could say, *"There is therefore now no condemnation to those who are in Christ Jesus, who do not walk according to the flesh, but according to the Spirit"* (Romans 8:1).

No blame. No censure. No black marks on your record. Because you trusted in God's Son, who gave His life for your salvation, your account has been stamped "Paid in Full!"

Here is how Paul explained the reason we are not condemned: *"For the law of the Spirit of life in Christ*

Jesus has made me free from the law of sin and death.
For what the law could not do in that it was weak
through the flesh, God did by sending His own Son in
the likeness of sinful flesh, on account of sin: He
condemned sin in the flesh, that
the righteous requirement of
the law might be fulfilled in us
who do not walk according to
the flesh but according to the
Spirit. For those who live
according to the flesh set their
minds on the things of the flesh,
but those who live according to
the Spirit, the things of the Spirit. (vv.2-5).

> **WE RECEIVE EVERY PROMISE OF THE FATHER BECAUSE WE PLACE OUR COMPLETE TRUST IN HIM.**

Every true Christian—those who unite with Him through the baptism of His Spirit—no longer remain under the penalty of sin.

Faith, Belief and Confidence

Do we have all the answers why God would provide a way for our escape? No. Can we understand how a just God would be so forgiving to an unjust world? Hardly. Yet we receive every promise of the Father because we place our complete trust in Him.

■ **With *faith* we experience redemption.**
"For by grace you have been saved

113

through faith, and that not of yourselves; it is the gift of God" (Ephesians 2:8).

■ **With *belief* we are free from condemnation.**
"He who believes in Him is not condemned; but he who does not believe is condemned already, because he has not believed in the name of the only begotten Son of God" (John 3:18).

■ **With *confidence* we can approach the Lord.**
"Now this is the confidence that we have in Him, that if we ask anything according to His will, He hears us" (1 John 5:14).

"In God We Trust"?

Millions spend sleepless nights filled with worry and anxiety. They are gripped with fear over issues ranging from failing finances, deteriorating health to rebellious children.

MILLIONS SPEND SLEEPLESS NIGHTS FILLED WITH WORRY AND ANXIETY.

The reason they are so overwhelmed and nervous is because they are relying on their own ingenuity to solve the problem. They "intellectualize" and depend only on their human abilities—not realizing there is a God in heaven ready and waiting to intervene on their behalf.

You see, relying on God is against our human

114

nature. Why? Because we think it is a sign of weakness—that we don't have control over our own destiny.

Americans have money in their pockets stamped with the words "In God We Trust," yet the only confidence they seem to have is in the almighty dollar!

When a physical problem surfaces, even before asking God for a miracle, people rush to the nearest hospital and place their total faith in the hands of a surgeon.

Do we exercise trust? Absolutely. We trust the airplane we board is going to take us safely to our destination—that our automobile is going to start tomorrow morning—the pill we take will make us feel better—that our employer is going to hand us a paycheck next week.

Where is Our Hope?

I can only imagine the revival that would sweep our nation if men and women would place as much hope and expectation in God as they do in science, government, law or education. Oh, the amazing patience of the Lord. He waits and waits for us to exhaust every ounce of our human resources before we finally, reluctantly call on Him.

Don't become intimidated or overwhelmed by the circumstances. While the thunder is still in the distance, begin to talk with the Lord. Then, as the storm clouds gather, start praising Him for the victory which is surely ahead. Say, "Lord, I don't have the answers. I am turning this problem over to You."

The Chariots are Coming!

Picture the scene. The children of Israel had fled Egypt, but soon found themselves in terrible trouble. On one side were the mountains, on the other was the sea—and coming toward them was Pharaoh's vast army. The Bible says he brought *"all the chariots of Egypt with captains over every one of them"* (Exodus 14:7).

As the approaching army was closing in, the terrified Israelites cried out to Moses, *"Why have you so dealt with us, to bring us up out of Egypt? Is this not the word that we told you in Egypt, saying, 'Let us alone that we may serve the Egyptians'? For it would have been better for us to serve the Egyptians than that we should die in the wilderness"* (vv.11-12).

Moses, however, had unswerving confidence in God. He answered the complaining throng, *"Do not be afraid. Stand still, and see the salvation of the Lord, which He will accomplish for you today. For the Egyptians whom you see today, you shall see again no more forever. The Lord will fight for you, and you shall hold your peace"* (vv.13-14).

That's when God made a way where there seemed no way! The waters of the sea parted and the children of Israel crossed on dry ground. Then, as Pharaoh's army pursued them, the great wall of water collapsed and the Egyptians drowned.

Much later, the psalmist wrote: *"Some trust in chariots, and some in horses; but we will remember the name of the Lord our God"* (Psalm 20:7).

> **GOD MADE A WAY WHERE THERE SEEMED NO WAY!**

Reasons for Trust

Let me give you ten reasons you can place your trust in God:

1. **He is your protector.** *"O Lord my God, in You I put my trust; save me from all those who persecute me; and deliver me"* (Psalm 7:1).
2. **He is your shield.** *"As for God, His way is perfect; The word of the Lord is proven; He is a shield to all who trust in Him"* (Psalm 18:30).
3. **He fulfills the desire of your heart.** *"Commit your way to the Lord, trust also in Him, and He shall bring it to pass"* (Psalm 37:5).
4. **He removes your fear**. *In God I have put my trust; I will not be afraid. What can man do to me?* (Psalm 46:11).

117

5. He is your refuge. *"The God of my strength, in whom I will trust...my shield and the horn of my salvation, My stronghold and my refuge; my Savior"* (2 Samuel 22:3).

6. He gives you wisdom. *"Trust in the Lord with all your heart, and lean not on your own understanding"* (Proverbs 3:5).

7. He is your deliverer. *"The Lord is my rock and my fortress and my deliverer; My God, my strength, in whom I will trust"* (Psalm 18:2).

8. He gives you mercy. *"Many sorrows shall be to the wicked; but he who trusts in the Lord, mercy shall surround him"* (Psalm 32:10).

9. He blesses your life. *"O Lord of hosts, blessed is the man who trusts in You!"* (Psalm 84:12).

10. He causes you to prosper. *"He who is of a proud heart stirs up strife, But he who trusts in the Lord will be prospered"* (Proverbs 28:25).

Where Will You Turn?

Don't be embarrassed to admit you do not have all the answers. Where will you turn when the storm is divorce, depression, or the death of a loved one?

Are we going to trust the power of man—or the

strength of Jehovah? Will we place our hope in the word of a stranger—or the Word of God?

I have made my decision. With Joshua I can say, *"...as for me and my house, we will serve the Lord"* (Joshua 24:15).

CHAPTER 10

THE BUTLER, THE BAKER, PHARAOH AND YOU

A God-given dream is more powerful than any storm you will ever encounter.

Joseph was a seventeen-year-old boy, working in the fields of his father, Jacob, when the Lord began working in his life. Did he have problems? Plenty of them—since Joseph was Jacob's favorite son and despised by the other brothers in the family. They were especially jealous of the fact their dad had given him "a coat of many colors" to wear.

The Bible records that Joseph had a dream and shared it with his brothers. He told them, *"Please hear this dream which I have dreamed: There we were, binding sheaves in the field. Then behold, my sheaf arose and also stood upright; and indeed your sheaves stood all around and bowed down to my sheaf"* (Genesis 37:6-7).

His brothers were indignant, responding, *"'Shall you indeed reign over us? Or shall you indeed have dominion over us?' So they hated him even more for his dreams and for his words"* (v.8).

Would They Bow?

This wasn't the end of the matter. Once more, Joseph shared with his brothers, *"Look, I have dreamed another dream. And this time, the sun, the moon, and the eleven stars bowed down to me"* (v.9).

Jacob heard what was taking place and rebuked his son, saying, *"What is this dream that you have dreamed? Shall your mother and I and your brothers indeed come to bow down to the earth before you?"* (v.10).

Scripture tells us his brothers envied Joseph, *"but his father kept the matter in mind"* (v.11). He thought, "Perhaps there just might be something to this!"

How could Joseph possibly know those same dreams were connected to the preservation of God's covenant people?

"The Dreamer is Coming!"

A few days later, after the brothers had gone to graze their father's flocks, Jacob asked Joseph to "Go and see if all is well—and bring me back a report."

Near a place called Dothan, the brothers saw Joseph approaching and said to each other, *"Look, this dreamer is coming! Come therefore, let us now kill him and cast him into some pit; and we shall say, 'Some wild beast has devoured him.' We shall see what will become of his dreams!"* (vv.19-20).

Their first step was to strip Joseph of his multi-colored tunic and throw him into an empty water pit.

Then as they sat down to eat lunch, the brothers looked up and saw a company of Ishmaelites headed for Egypt—their camels loaded with spices.

THE BROTHERS PULLED JOSEPH OUT OF THE PIT AND SOLD HIM AS A SLAVE FOR TWENTY SHEKELS.

One of the sons, Judah, spoke up and questioned, *"What profit is there if we kill our brother and conceal his blood? Come and let us sell him to the Ishmaelites, and let not our hand be upon him, for he is our brother and our flesh"* (vv.26-27).

As the traders passed by, the brothers pulled Joseph out of the pit and sold him as a slave for twenty shekels of silver. He was now headed for Egypt—where he was sold once more to Potiphar, the captain of Pharaoh's guard.

False Charges

God's hand rested on Joseph and *"made all he did to prosper"* (Genesis 39:4). Potiphar was so impressed with this handsome, well-built Hebrew, he made him overseer of everything he possessed.

Joseph's first storm in Egypt came when Potiphar's wife took notice of him and said, *"Lie with me"* (v.7).

He refused, yet day after day the woman pursued the young man. Once, Joseph went into the house to do his work when none of the other servants were present. Potiphar's wife *"caught him by his garment, saying, 'Lie with me.' But he left his garment in her hand, and fled and ran outside"* (vv.11-12).

Immediately, the woman summoned the men of the house and made a false charge. She accusingly said, "This Hebrew came here to mock us. He came here to lie with me and I screamed." She continued, *"...when he heard that I lifted my voice and cried out...he left his garment with me, and fled"* (v.15).

When Potipher returned and his wife showed him the "evidence," he became angry and threw Joseph into prison.

Even there, God showed him such favor the warden *"committed to Joseph's hand all the prisoners who were in the prison...and whatever he did, the Lord made it prosper"* (vv. 22-23).

You Need a Butler

Some time later, the butler and the baker of Pharoh offended the king and they, too, were thrown into the same prison where Joseph was confined. Ironically, Joseph was also placed in charge of these two men.

Friend, the Lord allows certain people in your life for a reason. Every dream needs a butler—an escort to take you where you need to go.

In the eye of the hurricane you may feel isolated and alone, yet God knows exactly where you are and what is required to see your vision fulfilled.

EVERY DREAMER NEEDS A BUTLER —AN ESCORT TO TAKE YOU WHERE YOU NEED TO GO.

I want you to know that, far in advance of your situation, the Father is preparing the right people at the right time for the right outcome. You may be in a deep dark valley, when, out of nowhere, a person appears to open a door for you to walk through. As we will see, this is exactly what the Lord did for Joseph.

Where is the Baker?

The second ingredient in dream fulfilment is someone who can help us stratigize and organize—putting the pieces together. This is where the baker comes in. To make a cake you need the correct mixture of flour, water, baking powder and shortening.

Your "baker" may be a friend who helps you write a business plan or an individual who can advise you on legal matters. Why is this person so important? Because without a sound, solid infrastructure, what you achieve may not withstand the storm.

Finally, You Need a Pharaoh

God can take a person of the world to fulfill your vision—either through finances, authority or decisions.

> **IF YOU ARE WALKING WITH GOD, HE CAN BRING ABUNDANCE FROM SOURCES YOU LEAST EXPECT.**

More often than not, we need a Pharaoh.

Many despise their boss, yet that man or woman in charge is giving them opportunities, promotions and funding their dream.

If you are walking with God, He can bring abundance from sources you least expect. The authority figure in your life may not be a believer, yet somehow God uses that individual to bless you. As the Bible declares, *"the wealth of the sinner is stored up for the righteous"* (Proverbs 13:22).

Three Branches

One day in prison, Joseph saw that both the butler

and the baker were dejected. "What's the problem," he asked them, *"Why do you look so sad today?"* (Genesis 40:7).

They replied, *"'We each have had a dream, and there is no interpreter of it.' So Joseph said to them, 'Do not interpretations belong to God? Tell them to me, please'"* (v.8).

The chief butler started first, telling Joseph details of his dream—where he saw a vine with three branches which were loaded with clusters of beautiful, ripe grapes. The butler continued, *"Then Pharaoh's cup was in my hand; and I took the grapes and pressed them into Pharaoh's cup, and placed the cup in Pharaoh's hand"* (v.11).

Joseph offered this interpretation: the three branches represented three days—the time it would take for Pharaoh to release the butler from prison and restore him to his former position in the household. And Joseph added, *"But remember me when it is well with you, and please show kindness to me; make mention of me to Pharaoh, and get me out of this house. For indeed I was stolen away from the land of the Hebrews; and also I have done nothing here that they should put me into the dungeon"* (vv.14-15).

Three Baskets

When the chief baker heard the positive interpretation, he also shared *his* dream—one where he saw three baskets on his head. In the top basket *"were all kinds of baked goods for Pharaoh, and the birds ate them out of the basket on my head"* (v.17).

Joseph interpreted the dream: *"Within three days Pharaoh will lift off your head from you and hang you on a tree; and the birds will eat your flesh from you"* (v.19).

Three days later was Pharaoh's birthday. At this celebration he restored the chief butler to his position, *"and he placed the cup in Pharaoh's hand. But he hanged the chief baker, as Joseph had interpreted to them"* (vv.21-22).

Unfortunately, the baker neglected to mention Joseph's plight. But this is not the end of the story.

Cows and Corn

Two years later, Pharaoh himself had two dreams. In the first, he saw seven fat cows come out of a river and begin feeding in a meadow. Then, seven "ugly and gaunt" cows came and ate the fine looking cows.

In the second dream, seven beautiful ears of corn came up on a stalk—then seven thin ears came up the stalk and devoured them.

The next morning Pharaoh's spirit was troubled and he called for all the magicians and wise men of Egypt, but no one could explain the dreams.

This is where the butler enters the scene. He told

Pharaoh how, in prison, a Hebrew man named Joseph had correctly explained the dreams of both he and the baker, *"And it came to pass, just as he interpreted for us, so it happened"* (Genesis 41:13).

Years of Plenty, Years of Famine

Immediately, Pharaoh called for Joseph to be brought out of the dungeon and said, *"I have had a dream, and there is no one who can interpret it. But I have heard it said of you that you can understand a dream, to interpret it"* (v.15).

Joseph answered Pharaoh, saying, *"It is not in me; God will give Pharaoh an answer of peace"* (v.16).

> **IMMEDIATELY, PHARAOH CALLED FOR JOSEPH TO BE BROUGHT OUT OF THE DUNGEON.**

After Pharaoh detailed the dreams of the cows and the corn, Joseph commented, "The two dreams are one—and God is showing you what He is about to do."

Joseph told him, *"Indeed seven years of great plenty will come throughout all the land of Egypt; but after them seven years of famine will arise, and...deplete the land"* (vv.29-30).

In addition, Joseph stated, *"Now therefore, let Pharaoh select a discerning and wise man, and set him over the land of Egypt...and let him appoint officers over the land, to collect one-fifth of the produce of the*

129

land of Egypt in the seven plentiful years. And let them gather all the food of those good years that are coming, and store up grain under the authority of Pharaoh, and let them keep food in the cities. Then that food shall be as a reserve for the land for the seven years of famine which shall be in the land of Egypt, that the land may not perish during the famine" (vv.33-36).

Pharaoh accepted the advice and said to his servants, *"Can we find such a one as this, a man in whom is the Spirit of God?"* (v.38).

You guessed it! Because the Lord had revealed Egypt's future, Pharaoh told Joseph, *"You shall be over my house, and all my people shall be ruled according to your word; only in regard to the throne will I be greater than you...I have set you over all the land of Egypt"* (vv.40-41).

Starving in Canaan

Now, at the age of 38, Joseph led the nation and administered a food conservation program during the seven years of abundance. Then the famine came—yet the storehouses were full. Suddenly, people from every country in the known world were coming to Joseph to buy grain.

Back in Canaan, Jacob's family was starving. So he sent his sons to Egypt to purchase supplies. Arriving before the governor—Joseph—the brothers *"came and bowed down before him with their faces to the earth"* (Genesis 42:6).

Joseph recognized them, but pretended to be a stranger, relishing the fact his dream as a 17-year-old boy had come true. The brothers not only bought supplies on their first journey, but returned again for more.

Preserving a Posterity

During this second trip, when they once again bowed before him, Joseph could not restrain himself. "Have everyone leave my presence," He cried out. *"So no one stood with him while Joseph made himself known. And he wept aloud"* (Genesis 45:2).

Then Joseph said to his brothers, *"'I am Joseph; does my father still live?' But his brothers could not answer him, for they were dismayed in his presence."* He continued, *"I am Joseph your brother, whom you sold into Egypt. But now, do not therefore be grieved or angry*

"I AM JOSEPH; DOES MY FATHER STILL LIVE?"

with yourselves because you sold me here; for God sent me before you...to preserve a posterity for you in the earth, and to save your lives by a great deliverance. So now it was not you who sent me here, but God; and He has made me a father to Pharaoh, and lord of all his house, and a ruler throughout all the land of Egypt" (vv.4 -5, 7-8).

Joseph Wept!

The brothers rushed back to Canaan and returned with their father Jacob—and all the relatives. What a reunion it was!

Pharaoh even gave the family the best land in Egypt where they settled. After Jacob died, and was returned to Canaan for burial, the brothers, fearing Joseph would repay them for their evil ways, sent him this word through messengers: *"Before your father died he commanded, saying, 'Thus you shall say to Joseph: I beg you, please forgive the trespass of your brothers and their sin; for they did evil to you. Now, please, forgive the trespass of the servants of the God of your father"* (vv.16-17).

Joseph wept when he received the message.

Next, his brothers also fell down before his face, and they said, *"Behold, we are your servants"* (v.18).

Joseph said to them, *"Do not be afraid, for am I in the place of God? But as for you, you meant evil against me; but God meant it for good, in order to bring it about as it is this day, to save many people alive"* (vv.19-20).

Keys to the Kingdom

All things work together for those who love the

Lord. This is why you should never fear a negative situation. When you look back, you'll see how it brought certain people into your life who became part of the solution.

In Joseph's story, it was a butler who opened the door to Pharaoh—the man who gave a Hebrew prisoner the keys to the kingdom.

You may despise the storm, but God means it for your good!

CHAPTER 11

YOUR ANCHOR IN AN ANGRY SEA

Suddenly, from the depths of the ocean, a giant earthquake caused a tidal wave beyond imagination.

It was Sunday morning, December 26, 2004, when the news broke that a tsunami had hit the Sumatra island of Indonesia. "Over 1,000 people may have been killed," announced the reporter. A short time later, the figure had risen to 3,000, then 6,000.

News flashes were coming in from all around the Indian Ocean—Thailand, Sri Lanka, India, Malaysia, and many islands. Entire villages were washed away and the death toll kept mounting. When it was over, we had witnessed one of the deadliest disasters in modern history, with over 200,000 people missing or killed.

"The Sea and Waves Roaring"

That Sunday, I opened my Bible and read once more

what Jesus said about the times before His Second Coming: *"Nation will rise against nation, and kingdom against kingdom. And there will be great earthquakes in various places, and famines and pestilences; and there will be fearful sights and great signs from heaven...And there will be signs in the sun, in the moon, and in the stars; and on the earth distress of nations, with perplexity, the sea and the waves roaring; men's hearts failing them from fear and the expectation of those things which are coming on the earth, for the powers of the heavens will be shaken. Then they will see the Son of Man coming in a cloud with power and great glory"* (Luke 21:10-11,25-27).

"LIFT UP YOUR HEADS, BECAUSE YOUR REDEMPTION DRAWS NEAR."

Earthquakes! Famines! The sea and waves roaring!

These are today's headlines, yet just over 2,000 years ago, Jesus declared, *"Now when these things begin to happen, look up and lift up your heads, because your redemption draws near"* (v.28).

If you know Christ as your Lord and Savior, you don't need to worry about the calamities of this earth. Why? *"Because we have "an anchor of the soul, both sure and steadfast"* (Hebrews 6:19).

A Dependable God

One of the great proclamations concerning a living

God on whom we can depend was made by the apostle Paul in Athens. He was in the city, waiting for Silas and Timothy to join him. However, the longer he walked around Athens the more angry he became. Everywhere he looked there were idols.

Each day he discussed the matter with the Jews, Gentiles and anyone else who happened to be nearby.

The Bible records, *"Epicurean and Stoic philosophers encountered him. And some said, 'What does this babbler want to say?' Others said, 'He seems to be a proclaimer of foreign gods,' because he preached to them Jesus and the resurrection"* (Acts 17:18-19).

The Epicureans followed the teachings of the Greek philosopher Epicures, who taught that happiness is found in gratification of the flesh.

The Stoics instructed people to recognize their independence and self-sufficiency—and to suppress desires. They preached purity and morality, but were so consumed with what they considered "right" they became overly judgmental.

PAUL WAS NOT INTIMIDATED BY THESE PEOPLE BECAUSE HE KNEW WHAT HE BELIEVED.

Paul was not intimidated by these people because he knew what he believed.

"We Want to Know"

The Athenians were intrigued and asked Paul to make

a presentation in the public area of the Areopagus. There, they asked, *"May we know what this new doctrine is of which you speak? For you are bringing some strange things to our ears. Therefore we want to know what these things mean"* (vv.20-21).

"MAY WE KNOW WHAT THIS NEW DOCTRINE IS OF WHICH YOU SPEAK?"

Paul stood before the people and spoke plainly concerning what he had observed. *"Men of Athens, I perceive that in all things you are very religious; for as I was passing through and considering the objects of your worship, I even found an altar with this inscription: TO THE UNKNOWN GOD"* (vv.22-23).

After capturing their attention, Paul presented the true and living God, saying, *"Therefore, the One whom you worship without knowing, Him I proclaim to you: God, who made the world and everything in it, since He is Lord of heaven and earth, does not dwell in temples made with hands. Nor is He worshiped with men's hands, as though He needed anything, since He gives to all life, breath, and all things"* (vv. 24-25).

"In Him We Live"

Paul explained how "from one blood," the Creator has made every nation of men on the earth—and has determined when and where they should live. God did this so they should seek the Lord and find Him, since *"He is not far from each one of us; for in Him we live and move and have our being"* (vv.27-28).

The apostle was saying, "If we are the creation of God, it doesn't make much sense to chisel a god out of stone—something of man's design."

Paul's life was filled with the reality of a living, breathing God. He wasn't like the men of Athens, worshiping without a relationship.

> **PAUL'S LIFE WAS FILLED WITH THE REALITY OF A LIVING, BREATHING GOD.**

Christ is the foundation of the world and the Rock on which we are secure—yet, we can know Him personally and commune with Him daily.

The Word Became Flesh

By receiving Christ, you are anchored to the Word.

The Gospel of John begins by declaring, *"In the beginning was the Word, and the Word was with God, and the Word was God. He was in the beginning with God. All things were made through Him, and without Him nothing was made that was made. In Him was life, and the life was the light of men. And the light shines in the darkness, and the darkness did not comprehend"* (John 1:1-5).

John's one purpose on earth was to testify of Jesus, He wrote, *"And the Word became flesh and dwelt among us, and we beheld His glory, the glory as of the only begotten of the Father, full of grace and truth"* (v.14).

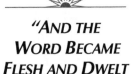

"AND THE WORD BECAME FLESH AND DWELT AMONG US."

A Solid Foundation

Because we have asked Christ to be our Lord and Savior we can stand on both the Living Word and the written Word of God.

Why is scripture such a reliable foundation? Let me give you 15 reasons:

1. The Word has power.

"For the Word of God is living and powerful, and sharper than any two-edged sword" ((Hebrews 4:12).

2. The Word builds our faith.

"So then faith comes by hearing, and hearing by the word of God" (Romans 10:17).

3. The Word provides spiritual growth.

"All Scripture is given by inspiration of God, and is profitable for doctrine, for reproof, for correction, for instruction in righteousness, that the man of God may be complete, thoroughly equipped for every good work" (2 Timothy 3:16-17).

140

4. The Word is incorruptible.

"...having been born again, not of corruptible seed but incorruptible, through the word of God which lives and abides forever" (1 Peter 1:23).

5. The Word makes us clean.

"...that He might sanctify and cleanse...with the washing of water by the word" (Ephesians 5:26).

6. The Word prepares our heart for salvation.

...from childhood you have known the Holy Scriptures, which are able to make you wise for salvation through faith which is in Christ Jesus" (2 Timothy 3:15).

"YOUR WORD HAVE I HIDDEN IN MY HEART, THAT I MIGHT NOT SIN AGAINST YOU."

7. The Word brings healing.

"He sent His word and healed them, and delivered them from their destructions" (Psalm 107:20).

8. The Word produces discipleship.

"If you abide in My word, you are My disciples indeed" John 8:31).

9. The Word keep us from iniquity.

"Your word I have hidden in my heart, that I might

not sin against You" (Psalm 119:11).

10. The Word protects us from Satan.
"Jesus said to him [the devil], It is written again, 'You shall not tempt the Lord your God'" (Matthew 4:7).

11. The Word is at work in the world.
"I am ready to perform My word" (Jeremiah 1:12).

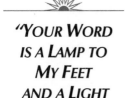

"YOUR WORD IS A LAMP TO MY FEET AND A LIGHT TO MY PATH."

12. The Word brings light.
"Your word is a lamp to my feet and a light to my path" (Psalm 119:105).

13. The Word gives life.
"For Your word has given me life" (Psalm 119:50).

14. The Word provides strength.
"My soul melts from heaviness; strengthen me according to Your word. (Psalm 119:28).

15. The Word is truth.
"Sanctify them by your truth. Your word is truth" (John 17:17).

Unmovable!

Don't risk the chance of being tossed by every wind

of doctrine or Satan's deceit. Become grounded in scripture until *nothing* can move you!

Follow the instructions of Solomon:

> *My son, give attention to my words;*
> *Incline your ear to my sayings.*
> *Do not let them depart from your eyes;*
> *Keep them in the midst of your heart;*
> *For they are life to those who find them,*
> *And health to all their flesh.*
> *– Proverbs 4:20-22*

Are you anchored in the Word?

CHAPTER 12

SOAR WITH THE EAGLES

I t's time to stretch your faith and abandon the mundane and ordinary and begin to embrace the supernatural life—at a level far beyond what you can ask or think.

When the Lord looks down from heaven, He does not see you as a person forever mired in problems. His image of you is one of victory and achievement. As He spoke through the prophet Isaiah, *"But those who wait on the Lord shall renew their strength; they shall mount up with wings like eagles, they shall run and not be weary, they shall walk and not faint"* (Isaiah 40:31).

Where are the "Eagle Christians?" I see very few. It seems the majority act like chickens—running in circles and following the crowd, squabbling and fighting, getting their feathers ruffled in the process.

If you've ever watched chickens, perhaps you have

noticed instead of lifting their head toward the sun, they seem quite content to keep their eyes focused on the ground, scratching for a morsel to eat. They have wings, yet never learn how to fly!

What a contrast to the eagle, perhaps the most majestic bird of the air. Its noble character is described in scripture: *"Does the eagle mount up at your command, and make its nest on high? On the rock it dwells and resides, on the crag of the rock and the stronghold. From there it spies out the prey; its eyes observe from afar"* (Job 39:27-29).

A Fresh Vision

The reason God desires for us to resemble eagles is not only so we can spread our wings and fly above the storm clouds, but to help perfect our vision.

The eagle is not just one of the fastest creatures in the sky, it has incredible eyesight. From as high as two miles, it can spot a tiny animal on the ground—then swoop down at over 100 miles an hour to snatch its prey.

Another amazing feature is their ability to see far more than a human with 20-20 vision. The eye of this great bird is the same diameter as man's, yet he can see four times as much.

How is this possible? The eagle has a membrane which comes down over the eye every two or three seconds, acting as a reflector. As a result of this extra "mirror," it can see in detail what is approaching from side to side. By just a turn of the head, it can view any danger from behind.

A Clear Revelation

I believe God develops Eagle Christians to make them sensitive to what is happening all around them—so Satan won't be able to launch a sneak attack.

The Lord also desires we have a revelation of hidden truth. The Bible tells us, *"Where there is no vision, the people perish"* (Proverbs 29:18 KJV). In the New King James Version it is translated, *"Where there is no revelation, the people cast off restraint"* (v.18).

In other words, without a vision there are no standards or discipline.

WITHOUT A VISION THERE ARE NO STANDARDS OR DISCIPLINE.

I believe the greatest revelation of God comes from your own experience. For example, you don't know how to be a compassionate doctor with empathy until you have been sick. You can't truly understand how to be a "friend who sticks closer than a brother" unless someone has hurt or abandoned you. In the words of David, *"When my father and my mother forsake me,*

147

then the Lord will take care of me" (Psalm 27:10).

If the vision for your future has yet to be revealed, stay before the Lord in prayer, and when it comes, be ready to start flying! The Lord told Habakkuk, *"Write the vision*

GOD HAS A VISION— A SPECIAL REVELATION JUST FOR YOU!

and make it plain on tablets, that he may run who reads it. For the vision is yet for an appointed time; but at the end it will speak, and it will not lie. Though it tarries, wait for it; because it will surely come, it will not tarry" (Habakkuk 2:2-3).

Yes, God has a special revelation just for you!

Eagle Strategies

If eagles could talk they would certainly tell us how to survive a blustery storm. Let me share three of their secrets:

1. Eagles fly best when winds are the strongest.

Perhaps you have seen an eagle circling effortlessly on a clear, sunny day. However, just wait for a strong breeze to start blowing and watch what happens. The bird will spread its wings and soar even higher.

The next time a problem is headed your way, don't panic. Look up to the Lord and say, *"You lift me up to the wind and cause me to ride on it"* (Job 30:22).

2. Eagles don't run and hide.

Practically every creature on earth will head for cover when the clouds turn black and the rain beats down. The eagle, however, actually challenges the storm. This is its finest hour— the chance to be strong and fly high.

THE EAGLE ACTUALLY CHALLENGES THE STORM.

3. Eagles use the sun as their compass.

The reason this regal bird can dive into a storm is because it does not plan to remain there. Instead of heading for the ground or a place of sanctuary, the eagle soars, breaking through the clouds where the sun is always shining.

When the tempest comes, say with the psalmist, *"I will lift up my eyes to the hills—from whence comes my help"* (Psalm 121:1).

New Wings

Three months after the children of Israel had departed from Egypt they came to Mount Sinai and camped in the wilderness in front of the mountain. For the first time on the journey, Moses had an encounter with God.

The message the Lord asked him to tell the people began with these words: *"You have seen what I did to the Egyptians, and how I bore you on eagles' wings and brought you to Myself"* (Exodus 19:4).

This was a reminder of what had transpired during the first 90 days of their dramatic exodus:

- They were led with a pillar of cloud by day and fire by night (Exodus 13:22).
- God parted the waters and allowed them to cross on dry ground (Exodus 14:29).
- The Egyptian army was swept into the sea (Exodus 14:28).
- By a miracle, the bitter water became sweet (Exodus 15:25).
- They were fed with manna from heaven (Exodus 16).
- The people drank from water which came out of a rock (Exodus 17:1-7).

Without question, the children had fled the tyranny of Pharaoh as if they had flown "on eagles' wings."

Up On the Mountain

Here is the rest of the message God asked Moses to tell the people: *"Now therefore, if you will indeed obey My voice and keep My covenant, then you shall be a special treasure to Me above all people; for all the earth is Mine. And you shall be to Me a kingdom of priests and a holy nation"* (Exodus 19:6-7).

Immediately, Moses announced what the Lord had said and the people answered together: *"All that the Lord has spoken we will do"* (v.8).

Something marvelous was about to happen and God wanted His people *consecrated!* The Lord told Moses, *"...let them wash their clothes. And let them be ready for the third day. For on the third day the Lord will come down upon Mount Sinai in the sight of all the people."* (vv.10-11).

On the morning of the third day, *"there were thunderings and lightnings, and a thick cloud on the mountain; and the sound of the trumpet was very loud, so that all the people who were in the camp trembled. And Moses brought the people out of the camp to meet with God, and they stood at the foot of the mountain"* (vv.16-17).

SUDDENLY, MOUNT SINAI WAS COMPLETELY COVERED IN SMOKE AS THE LORD DESCENDED UPON IT IN FIRE.

Suddenly, Mount Sinai was completely covered in smoke as the Lord descended upon it in fire. Then *"Moses spoke, and God answered him by voice"* (v.19)—calling Him to come up into the mountain. It was there he received the Ten Commandments.

Up on the mountain—where the eagle's make their nest—God chose to deliver His covenant with man.

Pass it On

It has been my prayer that what you have learned in this book will give you optimism and perseverance in the midst of your problem. Just as important, however, is that you share these principles with those you love.

> **IT'S ONE THING TO PROTECT OUR CHILDREN AGAINST A CRUEL, HARSH WORLD, YET IF THEY ARE EVER GOING TO BE CONFIDENT ON THEIR OWN, WE NEED TO TEACH THEM.**

We are fascinated when we see an eagle soar, yet they are at their best when taking care of their young.

The Bible paints this picture: *"As an eagle stirs up its nest, hovers over its young, spreading out its wings, taking them up, carrying them on its wings, so the Lord alone led him"* (Deuteronomy 32:11-12).

It's one things to protect our children against a cruel, harsh world, yet if they are ever going to be confident on their own, we need to teach them.

Flying Lessons

Imagine a family of eagles situated high on a cliff

with newborn eaglets hatched and flourishing in a safe, warm nest. This ideal scene doesn't last long. One day the mother "disturbs" the nest and, eventually destroys it—leaving the tiny ones to sleep on a bed of cold, hard rock. She is not being cruel; only preparing them for the real world.

Then the male will take the youngster out for flying lessons. Those who have watched the process are amazed. The father eagle will carry the fledgling on its back, circling in the sky. Then, suddenly, he will swoop away—letting the baby fall to see how well it flutters its wings.

Just before a disaster, the father eagle rushes down and rescues the bird out of the air and flies back home. This same process is repeated again and again until the baby eagle can make it on its own.

> *"MANY ARE THE AFFLICTIONS OF THE RIGHTEOUSNESS, BUT THE LORD DELIVERS HIM OUT OF THEM ALL."*

That's just like the Lord. He knows how you struggle, yet is watching and waiting to catch you when you fall.

In the words of the psalmist, *"The Lord is near to those who have a broken heart, and saves such as have a contrite spirit. Many are the afflictions of the righteous, but the Lord delivers him out of them all"* (Psalm 34:18-19).

You are His child—and He is teaching you how to

master the art of flying!

New Heights!

Starting today, become attuned to what the Lord is teaching you in your difficulties of life—large or small.

- Recognize the *purpose* in every storm you face.
- Never allow your spiritual ship to spring a leak.
- Look for opportunities to restore those who have fallen.
- Never create your own tempest.
- Cherish small storms, since they prepare you for a larger crisis.
- Ask the Lord to be your "safe house" and shelter.
- Mark out an "escape plan"—your path to deliverance in your darkest hour.
- Don't despair when you fail to have solutions—ask the Lord and He will answer.
- "Write the vision" and make it plain.
- Decide to soar above your storm.
- Never hesitate to say, "I need help!" God is always there.

While you have been reading this book, I believe the Lord is preparing you to reach new heights—to ride the rushing, mighty wind of the Spirit.

Since you have risen with Christ, seek those things which are higher—*"Set your mind on things above"* (Colossians 3:2).

You *will* survive your storm!

NOTES

_____

_____

_____

_____

_____

_____

_____

_____

_____

_____

_____

_____

_____

_____

_____

_____

_____

_____

FOR A COMPLETE LIST
OF RESOURCES BY THE AUTHOR,
OR TO SCHEDULE SPEAKING ENGAGEMENTS,
CONTACT:

LISTON PAGE, JR.
THE HIGHWAY CHURCH
371 10TH AVENUE
PATTERSON, NJ 07514

PHONE: 973-742-5118
OR 973-223-1681
EMAIL: highwaychurch@verizon.net
INTERNET: www.highwaychurch.org